Culture

at

Crisis Point

CULTURE
AT CRISIS POINT

GILES AUTY

Connor Court Publishing

Published in 2016 by Connor Court Publishing Pty Ltd

Connor Court Publishing Pty Ltd
PO Box 7257
Redland Bay QLD 4165

sales@connorcourt.com
www.connorcourt.com
Phone 0497 900 685

ISBN: 9781925501247

Front Cover Design: Maria Giordano

Front Cover Photo: Robert Billington

Printed in Australia

CONTENTS

INTRODUCTION

In spite of its slightly alarming title *Culture at Crisis Point* is intended to be a celebration of the joys of uninhibited thinking and writing as well as a source of possible remedies for at least some of our present, largely self-induced cultural, political and social ills.

When the human race behaves absurdly – as it does so regularly in many of the arts – I believe it is as well that someone is on hand sometimes at least to document such folly.

For in what other constructive way may we learn to move on from what is so often nothing more than sheer artistic pretentiousness?

Even outside the realm of the arts, human folly can often be almost as spectacular these days. Thus while *Dearth in Venice* (Chapter 43) recounts the all but incredible story of the 44th Venice Biennale, Chapter 17 chronicles idiocies in the policies of the European Union which are hardly less astonishing.

Unusually for someone who has latterly become a regular commentator on political, social and economic issues – no less than cultural ones – I spent the first significant phase of my life as a professional painter.

At the outset of that period I should admit I had very little idea even of how the visual arts themselves operated locally or nationally – let alone on an international basis.

However, working at the so-called coalface is probably as good a place as any to learn. In time, the somewhat credulous artist who once rode his motorbike each morning to an isolated painting studio in the wilds of rural Cornwall became an established cultural commentator who flew regularly out of London to cover a wide variety of overseas artistic events in more than twenty different countries.

Evidently such transitions do not happen overnight and Chapter 33 recounts the kind of personal discoveries which changed me, for instance, from being a person who was often confused by the assumed compulsions of time and fashion to becoming in time a battle-hardened observer who felt able to ignore such apparent pressures more or less completely.

While Chapters 31-43 look at some of the more extreme and unnecessary follies committed fairly recently in art's name, Chapters 11 to 30 – which basically form the core of this book – investigate subjects as diverse as military courage, atheism, multiculturalism, bushfires, racism, relativism, political correctness, pornography and professional sport.

I hope at least some of those subjects engage you.

Culture at Crisis Point is, in fact, basically a chronicle of personal discoveries such as the extraordinary way in which the precise meaning we attribute to a single word has influenced virtually a century of artistic practice in a highly detrimental fashion (Chapter 32) and why laws on so-called 'racism' may often conceal an entirely different agenda (Chapter 15).

Why then is it, given marked similarities in background, education and other variables do outwardly intelligent human beings seem to reach directly contrary conclusions so often?

The chapter with which I begin this book is based on a quotation from the rightly renowned book *Enemies of Promise* by English literary critic Cyril Connolly which was first published in 1938, shortly before the outbreak of the Second World War: "Within his talent it is the duty of a writer to devote his energy to the search for truth, the truth that is always being clouded over by romantic words and ideas or obscured by actions and motives dictated by interest and fear. In the love of truth which leads to a knowledge of it lies not only the hope of humanity but its safety".

Later in the same piece Connolly writes: "A writer can help to liberate that knowledge and to unmask those pretenders which accompany all human plans for improvement: the love of power and money, the short-sighted acquisitive passions, the legacies of injustice and ignorance, the tiger instinct for fighting, the ape-like desire to go with the crowd. A writer must be a lie-detector who exposes the fallacies in words and ideals before half the world is killed for them".

During the darkest moments of the Second World War, Connolly edited the literary magazine *Horizon* which upheld the highest standards of culture during those most unpromising of times. Why then are we so apparently effete now that we seem generally incapable of creating or maintaining anything of comparable literary worth or relevance today?

I was already alive and a member of a somewhat unusual household when the unforgettable words of Connolly quoted above were first written.

At that time my scholarly father was an impecunious schoolmaster who had recovered only recently from a serious illness. Our house, on the outskirts of a small English country town in Kent, was full to the rafters with books but boasted very little else of value. In the meantime my earliest schooling was interrupted by being evacuated twice because our house lay in the direct path of a possible German invasion.

However as soon as I had gained some proper mastery of reading my literary appetites rapidly became unusually adult – as well as voracious – in nature since there were virtually no children's books in our home. Thus a large part of my early reading consisted rather strangely of such unlikely material as early 20th century and Victorian poetry and the Icelandic sagas in translation.

What do you personally know about the deeds of Erik Blood-Axe?

That – along with the poetry of T.S. Eliot – was the kind of thing I was reading regularly by the age of ten.

I also began learning Latin at home from the age of eight and started French the following year when I gained a place somewhat prematurely at a local grammar school.

Most of my childhood friends, including a cousin who has died recently in New Zealand, were being groomed at that time to try to gain admission to King's School, Canterbury. That ancient, famous and truly excellent school included among its fairly recent luminaries the extraordinary writer and adventurer Patrick Leigh Fermor – but perhaps typically he was expelled.

In spite of my unusually extensive reading however I was by no means the bespectacled 'swot' beloved of fiction but was a thoroughly athletic and sports-loving boy. Indeed, because my rather older cousin and I fought physically whenever our unfortunate parents met to play bridge it was decided that if my cousin were accepted by King's School, Canterbury that I should be sent elsewhere.

My father, who was the son of a schoolmaster himself, had won a scholarship as a boarder to a school in Essex named Bancroft's which was founded by the Worshipful Company of Drapers. Apparently he had generally loathed the experience in spite of being appointed – as I later was – that school's captain of cricket.

However with the rather perverse logic not unusual at the time I was shortly entered for a scholarship as a boarder at that self-same school myself. With the somewhat inflated size of the vocabulary at my disposal already, I probably passed the entrance exams very easily indeed although rather younger than most of my competitors.

At the age of ten I therefore found myself shortly obliged to leave home more or less for good – a singular circumstance which possibly bred in me a somewhat premature development of independence of mind, a characteristic which has certainly remained with me.

In time my late father took early retirement from teaching and pursued his true professional love instead: etymology. Quite soon after that, in fact, he became a senior reader for the Complete Oxford English Dictionary, contributing some 26,000 original entries to that publication's 1970 supplement.

Such intellectual skills apart, few more impractical and eccentric people than my late father may ever have existed.

Even the most elementary practical task such as changing a light bulb defeated him yet in his day he was a fine left-handed cricketer who played in the famous Staffordshire league with various future immortals of the game.

He, in turn, taught me to catch, bowl and throw hard and very accurately from an early age. Indeed, as rather an unlikely result of his input I flattened a fellow boarder with an acorn on my very first day at boarding school. If I had been born a generation later – when pay was much more generous – I suspect I might even have been tempted by a career in professional cricket myself.

Sporting abilities aside I have always been divided more or less evenly between joint desires to paint and write. Indeed for most of the first twenty years of my adult life I had little expectation of ever being anything other than a professional painter – even though I generally wrote for an hour or so at the conclusion of each day's work in the studio.

However it was possibly only through the most unlikely good fortune that the daily notes I wrote became published later on in book form at the precise moment when other dissident voices about the state of modern art were first becoming heard widely on an international stage.

Indeed, the increasingly bizarre excesses of late modernism had attracted the attention of writers as various as Tom Wolfe in America (*The Painted Word*), noted Picasso scholar Helene Parmelin in France(*Art anti Art: Anartism Explored*) and art historian Vladislav Zimenko in the former Soviet Union(*The Humanism of Art*). At the time I was by some lengths the least known of the quartet.

However, an extremely generous review by Patrick Marnham in the pages of *The Spectator* of what amounted basically to my rather ill-assembled thoughts was later to change the direction of my life in ways I could never have foreseen. I write about the consequences of his generous review in Chapter 30.

Indeed, even before those consequences happened, the publication of my book *The Art of Self Deception* had already helped gain me a very convenient part-time teaching post at an art school near London. It was just before that job finally ended, in fact, that I began a long and happy association with *The Spectator* the weekly for which I subsequently wrote some 500 articles and book reviews over the course of the next eleven years.

Invitations to write for other well-known magazines such as

Apollo and Modern Painters shortly followed my appointment as did an invitation to join the Conservative Advisory Committee for the Arts and Heritage on which I served for some years as visual arts spokesman. In 1990-91 I was further invited to join The Art Working Group for the National Curriculum for English and Welsh Schools which introduced me at first hand to the kind of dilemmas which beset the teaching of art to younger-aged students. It was widely believed my appointment to that Working Group was initiated by then British Prime Minister Margaret Thatcher.

While working for *The Spectator* I filed reports on art from more than twenty different countries and was lucky enough to visit many of the world's great art collections, at least some of which were previously unknown to me. The finest exhibition I have ever seen took place at the Prado Museum in Madrid in February 1990 and featured nearly eighty works by Diego Velazquez (Chapter 42) an incomparable and absolutely unforgettable show which I contrast with the sheer silliness of the Venice Biennale which took place slightly later that same year (Chapter 43).

By now sadly what pass for standards in contemporary art are ruled also by the frequent absurdities of the marketplace. For example, just last year thirty odd crudely stencilled letters on a sheet of aluminium changed hands for $26 million US. This was Apocalypse Now 'by' American artist Christopher Wool who simply quoted some mutterings by the deranged officer from the famous film of that name. Wool is just one of the highly fashionable artists I discuss unfavourably in Chapter 10.

How then have we managed to relapse from the sublime levels of skill and beauty reached by 17th century painters such as Velazquez, Rembrandt and Vermeer to the kind of nonsense represented by Wool's offerings today?

And who else is remarking regularly today on the widespread collapse of human culture which is continuing to take place under our very noses?

Culture at Crisis Point presents a world view which a commentator for the ABC, for instance, might possibly characterise as merely idiosyncratic yet which was and is shared by a very large number of intelligent people worldwide.

So who then are or should be the keepers of our notions of artistic or moral worth or basic commonsense?

Not long after I came to Australia to work in 1995, a friend of mine was asked by a prominent ABC radio interviewer to suggest some possible new names for her show.

When my name was mentioned she replied very indignantly: "I can't possibly have people like that on my show".

What precisely did she mean by that?

Total intolerance of alternative views does not sit particularly well in my mind where any public broadcaster is concerned.

The arts in Australia desperately need international input if they are to make genuine progress rather than simply to stagnate or decline.

What *Culture at Crisis Point* may ultimately represent, in fact, is the overdue exposure of views which seek to question and overthrow the myopic nature of at least some of the prevailing orthodoxies which rule the roost today not just in Australia itself but in far too much of the rest of the developed world.

Our culture, in the word's broadest sense, needs belatedly to rediscover some sense of having a backbone – for the sorry alternative is nothing less than the long-term collapse of vital areas of civilisation itself.

1

WAKE-UP CALL FROM A WISER AGE

A while ago after finally unpacking several hundreds of my books which had previously lacked shelf-space, I re-read Cyril Connolly's *Enemies of Promise* for the first time in about 20 years.

Connolly's acknowledged masterpiece of literary criticism was first published in 1938 and re-issued in 1973 by Andre Deutsch on the occasion of its author's 70th birthday.

During my own formative years as a writer, I read Connolly's literary reviews regularly in English newspapers yet had forgotten somehow, over the intervening period, just what an incisive and humorous mind Connolly possessed.

I began my own career as a professional writer in the year Connolly died – 1974 – and have no grounds for claiming him then or now as any kind of direct influence. Yet re-reading him recently was such a pleasure that I could not help wishing I had met him, however briefly, because of the sense of delighted agreement I felt with so many of his arguments and judgements – especially so perhaps about the merits and demerits of Marcel Proust.

Evidently, like everyone else on this planet, writers cannot choose the precise era or circumstances into which they are born.

While I can have no argument with the latter I still cannot help regretting sometimes that I missed out, as a professional writer, on the experience of the inter-war years.

In spite of the Depression and the darkening shadow of a second world conflict, there seemed a sense of seriousness combined with hope not only among writers generally but also just as significantly among many of their publishers. Excellent writing still seemed to matter profoundly to both parties then as did what Connolly described aptly as a writer's 'duty to the truth'.

Perhaps no other pair of factors can epitomise more clearly the depth of difference between writing 70 years ago and trying to write today.

While a general decline in the seriousness of some publishers was possibly foreseeable, I doubt whether Connolly or anyone else could ever have foreseen the concerted attack on the idea of singular truth which has been unleashed during the post-modern era. Indeed, Connolly may thus have avoided a good deal of disillusionment by dying when he did.

Why is the idea of singular truth so distasteful to a post-modernist audience?

In the grey-hued hinterland known as relativism, a worrying confusion seems to me to exist at an absolutely elementary level between the unrelated concepts of truth and opinion. This is an especially damaging confusion because while truth can evidently influence opinion, opinion as such can have no umbilical or other bearing on truth.

In short, truths can and do exist which are totally unacknowledged by anyone to date. One needs think no further here than matters of future scientific or medical discovery.

However, the discipline which possibly provides the best examples of the fundamental difference between truth and opinion is archaeology. What archaeology provides *par excellence*, in fact, are examples of literally hidden and buried truths.

What I like especially about the latter is the clarity with which they demonstrate that truth is in no way dependent on the opinions even of experts. Thus the world's greatest experts may believe that some historic site is located in such and such an area yet clearly may or may not be right in their suppositions. Therefore until proved to be so or not by incontestable evidence both the riddle and factual truth itself about where the actual location is simply remain. In short, even if nobody ever discovers the truth about where an actual site is located *a truth evidently exists about that which is utterly independent of human opinion.*

Archaeologists may exist admittedly who seek to advance their careers through ill-advised expressions of opinion yet clearly risk, by doing so, some possibility of being proved utterly wrong. A career in archaeology thus seems to me to stand at the furthest possible remove from one in today's so-called 'communications' industry. While the former involves the digging up of buried truths, the latter too often involves the burying of dug-up truths via political spin or what is referred to euphemistically today as 'public relations'.

Worthwhile criticism – or so it seems to me – involves aiding the reader or, in my former case, viewer to understand what the writer or artist is trying (or failing) to do. A grasp of and profound knowledge of history is vital to such a task, if for no other reason than the sense of perspective that provides. Critics of any of the arts should carry in their minds a list of supreme practitioners and be able at all moments to justify such choices clearly. Yet long before critics can explain complex issues to their readers a competence must exist to explain such issues clearly to themselves. Here is yet another reason why re-reading Cyril Connolly in a world abuzz with the vacuities of post-modernist theory remains so revitalising and deeply refreshing to the soul.

Here are a few of the thoughts Connolly penned in those darkest of days shortly before the outbreak of the Second World War: "Within his talent it is the duty of a writer to devote his energy to the search for truth, the truth that is always being clouded over by romantic words and ideas or obscured by actions and motives dictated by interest and fear. In the love of truth which leads to a knowledge of it lies not only the hope of humanity but its safety. Deep down we feel that, as every human being has a right to air and water, so has he a right to food, clothing, light, heat, work, education, love and leisure. Ultimately we know the world will be run, its resources exploited and its efforts synchronised on this assumption. A writer can help to liberate that knowledge and to unmask those pretenders which accompany all human plans for improvement: the love of power and money, the short-sighted acquisitive passions, the legacies of injustice and ignorance, the tiger instinct for fighting, the ape-like desire to go with the crowd. A writer must be a lie-detector who exposes the fallacies in words and ideals before half the world is killed for them".

Those wise words were written more than seventy years ago.

But who on earth else still writes about 'searching for truth' today?

Annals, May 2015

2

CRITICAL ISSUES

During those happy days when I was as likely to be found on a plane to Paris or Venice as on an express train heading to Edinburgh I soon learned not to discuss what the purpose of my trip was or what my role might be when I arrived at my destination.

That was so that I might not get involved in a conversation either with the IT expert seated on my right or the financial consultant seated to my left about the possible purposes of art criticism – nor feel obliged to respond for the umpteenth time to the following question: "Surely all art criticism is simply a matter of subjective opinion?"

Over the preceding years I had indeed formulated a number of responses to this tiresome query but found these often relied too much on my questioner's knowledge – or lack of it – regarding art history.

That said the general purpose answer I favour is this: "If you take six centuries of European art from the time of Giotto to the death of Gauguin in 1903 you will find there is a huge consensus among experts about who the truly outstanding artists were and who were merely the also-rans. So kindly tell me whether that overwhelming consensus is just a matter of pure coincidence or one of a covert conspiracy among international scholars".

The true essence of the matter is this: violent disagreement among so-called experts about the respective merits of artists does not really get under way until we start to deal with those artists active principally from the beginning of the 20th century onwards e.g. from about the time of the first Fauve exhibition in 1906.

Thus if we apply the largely aesthetic criteria by means of which many of us consider Giotto, Leonardo, Titian, Rembrandt, Velazquez, Vermeer, Goya, Constable, Manet and van Gogh, say, to be utterly remarkable artists how then may we apply exactly the same critical criteria to Marcel Duchamp, Jackson Pollock, Andy Warhol or Joseph Beuys – let alone to Jeff Koons or Damian Hirst – and then consider them similarly to be great artists?

The short answer is that we can do no such thing; it is only by altering the qualities thought vital for outstanding artistic excellence more or less entirely – for example by trying to make mere novelty a virtue in itself – that we can even begin to come up with such a result.

I preface my words about the last published anthology of Brian Sewell's art criticism *Naked Emperors* (Quartet Books 2012) in this manner simply to establish a few ground rules not just regarding Brian's excellent book but also about the dilemmas which face contemporary art in general.

Both Brian and I began our mainstream critical careers in 1984: in his case at London's *Evening Standard* and in mine with *The Spectator.* Inevitably our paths crossed very frequently before I came to Australia to work in 1995. To state that Brian was a highly respected rival rather than a particular friend merely reflects a divergence in our extra-mural activities because in terms of art criticism and reasoned argument I was and remain a paid-up admirer of one of the last true – and utterly fearless – defenders of lasting artistic values.

Naked Emperors contains 30 often lengthy articles involving criticisms of English contemporary art. In general these are as remarkable for their high-flying prose as for their biting and often hilarious wit.

The presence of wit is especially vital to the book because much of what Sewell describes might otherwise seem deeply depressing. Yet the essays all deal with figures proposed by other critics from our present thickheaded age as being thoroughly deserving of national and international fame.

While some of the artists described in the anthology will probably be unfamiliar to Australian audiences, the issues with which Sewell deals are fundamentally universal as well as timeless.

Of course, working in close proximity to Europe and not too far from America makes it much easier for British critics to base their beliefs on a deep knowledge of international collections and masterpieces in a way that is impossible for most critics based in Australia.

Brian is therefore justifiably rude about the host of British and European critics who betray the knowledge readily available to them by buying into 'equivalence' theories which are fundamentally completely false. Thus Sewell is right to ridicule the notion encouraged by authorities from the Royal Academy of Arts in London in 2001, for instance, that Frank Auerbach is somehow 'a Rembrandt of our times' by deliberately exhibiting an earnest but somewhat limited artist at the same moment as one of the greatest masters who ever lived. Such 'equivalence' arguments represent false reasoning at its worst yet are very popular indeed – it hardly needs saying – with the ambitious dealers who represent fashionable contemporary artists.

The total lie is given to such silly arguments, of course, when 'the real thing' is so often available to be seen either in London itself or in nearby continental Europe.

To his great credit, Sewell carries in his mind an exhaustive list of artists from previous times whose achievements make the pretensions of over-praised artists from the present seem ludicrous at best. Thus, writing about Howard Hodgkin whom too many now propose as some kind of 'modern master', Sewell has the following to say: "Since late June thirteen paintings by Howard Hodgkin have been hanging in Dulwich Picture Gallery. They are not confined to a single room, there to be venerated in a cataleptic trance; they are instead scattered among the distinguished pictures in the permanent collection, rubbing shoulders with Poussin, Ricci and Guercino, keeping company with Claude, Rubens and Rembrandt, illuminating all – or so we are told – the juxtaposition leading to our greater understanding of the present and the past, Hodgkin and his wonderful precursors speaking the same language. That is the official way of perceiving this chalk and cheese display."

Later from the same article he adds: "It is, of course, just possible that Dulwich is being subtle, guileful and subversive, its intention quite the reverse of what at first it seems – that Dulwich is, in fact, demonstrating how fatuous and vacuous contemporary art can be by hanging a sloppy Hodgkin between a pair of Poussins that we all know to be monuments of scrupulously careful pictorial construction, the contrast made perhaps to reassure the visitor who perceives the work of Hodgkin as pretentious trash".

Probably the names of David Hockney, Lucian Freud, Damian Hirst, Tracey Emin and Gilbert & George will be more familiar even to expert audiences here than that of Howard Hodgkin and all are given a varied but largely justified degree of come-uppance in Sewell's book. After all Hockney and Freud have large and extremely ill-chosen works in the National Gallery of Australia where they bear witness to the general cluelessness of former directors of that institution.

I was in London when the vast exhibition AUSTRALIA, largely sourced from the NGA, struck the Royal Academy there with all the force of a much downgraded cyclone and Sewell was one of the many critics there to give it the thumbs-down. London is a much more sophisticated city now than when the 1961 exhibition of Australian art at the Whitechapel Gallery awoke many to the originality and insouciance of artists such as Nolan, Boyd and Whiteley. Very sadly for me since I am now a dual passport holder, AUSTRALIA was widely considered by senior British critics to be the worst major public exhibition in London of its year.

How, with the considerable resources at its organisers' disposal, could such an entirely unnecessary travesty occur?

Sewell's book describes with great force how the development of 'state' art in Britain and of bossy but often clueless or corrupt ancillary funding bodies have combined to usher in decades there of generally worthless 'official' state art.

Indeed, Sewell describes Britain's Arts Council, possibly too kindly, as "a nest of vipers". I first locked horns with that body myself, to my professional disadvantage, way back in the 1970s. Sewell's book is therefore not without relevance to Australia where similar institutions exist thus helping render this country incapable of representing itself either appropriately – or fairly – on an international stage. Consider for a moment just some of the bizarre or atrocious choices made to 'represent' Australia as a whole at prestigious international events such as Venice Biennales and you will begin to see what I mean.

Today's problems of art are international because they arise from the same or similar sources. That is why Sewell's hugely entertaining book is one everyone with a true interest in the subject should make a strenuous effort to purchase and read.

Here is simply another sentence, drawn at random from the book, regarding a typical 'state art' occasion held at London's Tate Gallery: "There is, in this exhibition, not one single work of interest or merit. These are paintings that say with drip, splash and sweep of the brush:

> "Look, look, I am a painting" – but drip, splash and sweep
> of the brush are merely marks that reflect the physical action
> of the painter and, meaningless without intelligent purpose,
> are not enough to make a painting".

Do you feel, at this moment, some inclination to rise up from your chair and cheer?

When I first started out in art – as a painter – it was fashionable both in Britain and elsewhere to poke fun at the official state art of the former Soviet Union which frequently featured 'heroic' tractor drivers or wives bidding last farewells to Red Army patriots setting forth to defend their 'motherland'.

I was probably one of the first people in Britain to source and buy a book about such art: Vladislav Zimenko's *The Humanism of Art* published by Progress Publishers in Moscow. Its author signed my copy a dozen or so years later in Moscow's Arts Club.

Here was, indeed, an example of art totally controlled by the state – indeed all too obviously so.

In its favour, the artists involved generally underwent a six year training of a traditional nature which included courses in anatomy or – in the cases of sculptors – in the carving of marble. How many students do either in Western art schools today?

Little did we imagine, nearly half a century ago, that official 'state' art – of a more informal nature admittedly – would similarly rear its head in most Western democracies. Yet no Russian arts commissar probably ever achieved the power of contemporary figures in Britain such as Nicholas Serota at the Tate Gallery who effectively enjoys the 'thumbs up/thumbs down' powers there of a Roman Emperor.

Instead of gladiatorial contests, however, Britain's unfortunate public is treated to such meaningless non-contests as the annual Turner Prizes which belong more properly, perhaps, in overtly totalitarian North Korea.

Sewell is as scathing as I ever was about such non-events : "It hardly matters who is chosen for the short list (though sceptics believe this to be decided long before the year is out), or to whom the large prize is given by the judges, for the real and far larger arena is not within Tate Britain, but in the press, the media, the fashionable watering-holes of Islington and the mahogany dining tables of Tunbridge Wells. In all these quarters the Prize is seen as a Brueghelian bout between drunken Carnival and sober Lent, blind Folly and dumb Wisdom, so weighted in favour of the Serota Tendency that Carnival and Folly always win".

At the time even of contemplating writing this article Brian has been desperately ill. Should he not survive I wish to pay a personal tribute to the man who, as a dissident voice, has probably contributed more than any other to keeping the causes of sanity and scholarship alive in British art although the critic David Lee, editor and founder of the magazine *The Jackdaw*, would run him a close second.

The Jackdaw has just reprinted a very lengthy essay I wrote for *Quadrant* in April 2006 on the grounds that it explains the highly complex dilemmas of Modernism in terms that anyone interested in the subject can readily understand.

In *The Spectator* of 17 February 1996, the eminent historian and worthy amateur artist Paul Johnson was kind enough to include me among "only four outstanding art critics in Britain in the previous forty years" and I refer to this now only to take issue with one of his other inclusions: John Berger.

The other two art critics he named were Peter Fuller and Brian Sewell.

As a former Marxist, Fuller awoke late to the menace inherent in Berger's theories and most of Fuller's published books chart his growing disillusionment with Berger and his belated discovery of the merits of the 19th century English critic John Ruskin. Fuller was unfortunately killed in a motor accident 25 years ago but was never, in my view, the possessor of a 'good eye'. In other words his aesthetic judgements were often fallible.

As a critic Berger was a strange paradox: the possessor of excellent aesthetic instincts which could easily find themselves swamped by his lifelong devotion to Marxist causes.

Berger's vast former influence gave rise forty years ago to a school of so-called 'social' critics devoted to 'Marxist analysis' and to a belief that art should be judged for its social or political influence rather than by its intrinsic merit *as art*. A corollary to this ultra-destructive view was that 'aesthetic' values were somehow a 'bourgeois' myth – a means, in fact, whereby a privileged social class could impose its tastes on less privileged ones.

The so-called 'culture wars' feature this kind of issue prominently, of course, but if we substitute the words 'well-educated' for the word 'privileged' a rather different complexion emerges rather rapidly.

Almost all the atrocious art movements of the past forty years – such as 'conceptualism' – arose from political theory. In the latter case through the idea that if commercial dealers could be deprived of physical objects with which to trade that this would hasten the desired demise of capitalism. So art should be reduced basically simply to the 'idea' e.g. a phial of the water in which the artist bathed while ruminating about his or her world-shattering ideas. This was all that was needed as 'evidence'.

Essentially Sewell and I are 'aesthetic' critics who would be happy to write long essays on the superiority of Titian to, say, Jacopo Bassano – a brilliant and original painter in his own right – if anyone might still show any interest in reading such things.

But who else is still interested in proper standards of criticism or scholarship today?

Quadrant, August 2015

3

A DUCK-BILLED PLATYPUS OF A SHOW

So far the giant exhibition AUSTRALIA which is up and hopping now at the Royal Academy seems to have confused many people – possibly including those responsible for organising it in the first place.

The real problem with the show is a simple confusion of aims: in short was this meant to be an exhibition of stunning and unforgettable Australian art or more of a history lesson for the remaining handful of people who may not be entirely sure who Charles Darwin, William Bligh and Ned Kelly were?

If a camel is a horse designed by a committee what occurs when an all-Australian group drawn almost all from the same institution – the National Gallery of Australia – and seeing each other every day set about devising a vast show for an overseas location?

A bit of outside or even foreign input could have brought in not just a necessary sense of perspective but a very welcome breath of fresh air.

Huge shows such as this should be part of London's entertainment programme rather than what can amount in the end to an institutionalised historical plod. The whole basis of the show should have been much more ruthlessly selective – but that takes skills which are in increasingly short supply these days thanks, in part, to the widespread politicisation of critical thinking which had its origins with John Berger.

In short many now tend to ask whether a work of art is politically acceptable long before questioning whether it is any good at all.

Australia has produced some truly remarkable artists but by no means all of them feature in this 200 year history show. In the preview I wrote in the July/August edition of *The Jackdaw* I mentioned three artists of international standard who are virtually unknown outside their native shores. All three are likely to remain so because each is represented very inadequately here by just a single picture.

Indeed, in the case of one of the more brilliant draughtsmen in the entire history of Western art – the late Lloyd Rees – the artist is represented absurdly by a tiny grey, almost anonymous painting. Rees went through an extraordinary period in the 1930s when he produced lyrical pencil drawings which bear interesting comparison with our own Samuel Palmer's famous Shoreham pictures from 100 years earlier. But who will ever learn about any of that now?

In the cases of John Olsen and William Robinson both are at least represented by a painting of reasonable size although both find themselves lumped in with some very forgettable artists indeed in the strangely-named section *Elizabethan Post-Colonial 1950-2013* which forms one of the five sections of the show.

Olsen used to mutter to me regularly about Australian curators whose eyes, in his view, were located in entirely the wrong part of their anatomies – thus impeding their vision seriously whenever they sat down.

Robinson is an infinitely more accomplished and imaginative painter of large landscapes than David Hockney as even a quick glance at his solitary work in AUSTRALIA will confirm. If someone put together an in-depth show of works by Rees, Olsen and Robinson under a title such as Romantic Landscape Down Under and supplemented these with batches of work by such as the late Kenneth Macqueen – another absolutely world-class Australian artist, also represented here by just a small solitary work – the show could indeed bring something utterly remarkable and truly memorable to London.

But what are the chances of that happening? I am tempted to howl sometimes from sheer frustration. The other four sections of AUSTRALIA feature Aboriginal Art, The Colonial Encounter 1800-1880, Australian Landscape 1880-1920 and lastly The Modern World 1920-1950.

Many of the delightful topographical paintings of the second section are small in size and predominantly green in colour so that the decision to hang them in a low-slung line on high walls painted a uniform shade of very dark green certainly seems an odd one. Indeed because they are also lit somewhat dimly from very highly-placed lights I even worried briefly about my eyesight. If I failed to recognise any old friends from overseas in the all-pervading gloom please accept my apologies.

The third section dating from 1880-1920 features some very solid painting by such as Tom Roberts, George Lambert and Arthur Streeton. Roberts certainly knew about Jules Bastien-Lepage in France and brought home the influence of the latter to Australia's shores, thus replicating the latter's influence in lands which also include England, Scotland, Scandinavia, Italy, Russia and the United States. This influence also led to the setting up of outdoor artists' camps and artists' colonies in all of those countries but had nothing at all to do with the use of fragmented colour by the Impressionists. No remotely educated person therefore thinks of Newlyn School artists such as Stanhope Forbes as Impressionists and that word should now cease forever to be applied to their Australian counterparts also. Here is an art historical solecism of the first degree.

The most beautiful and accurate rendition of Australian light in the whole show can be found in Lambert's *The Squatter's Daughter* 1923-24. The sketches and paintings Lambert made some years earlier as a war artist are also among the finest such made anywhere in the world. But these can prove difficult to see even in Australia.

Why were these not included?

The fourth section of the show brings us to names and works which are almost over- familiar even in Britain where Arthur Boyd and Sidney Nolan both chose to spend the latter parts of their lives. Nolan was a hugely prolific, very uneven but sometimes inspired artist while Boyd latterly churned out facile images of the Shoalhaven river like an out of control machine. But luckily he was a thoroughly interesting and significant artist long before that.

Nolan's Ned Kelly series is rightly famous and iconic but also regrettably represents an aspect of Australia which has never quite gone away: endemic violence and corruption.

Whether that aspect of Australia should still be romanticised may strike some as questionable. To date no-one has produced a series of works featuring the widows of the policemen slaughtered by Kelly but even if they did I doubt any such would make the front cover of the catalogue as well as a great deal of the publicity for what is intended to be a prestigious national show.

Happily much that is latent in Australia will be unseen and unnoticed by you on the idyllic five week holiday you may shortly decide to spend in that country.

The recent history of the art of any country should never be set in stone. I contend that Olsen, Rees and Robinson are as significant as any trio of 20th century Australian artists drawn from the ranks of Nolan, Boyd, Tucker, Drysdale, Williams and Whiteley, say, all of whom tend to be more renowned than my trio both at home and abroad.

I had not heard of Olsen, Rees and Robinson at all when I first went to Australia and brought a fresh set of eyes to bear on the art of that land.

One final point here is that a man who may well be Australia's most sought-after living artist, Tim Storrier, does not make this show at all.

A very large work by Storrier at his best – of a comet, say, passing over an Australian desert at night – could be thought to personify a perfectly valid experience of that vast continent. But do not even whisper this: Storrier is a staunch political conservative who dresses and behaves rather like an English squire. He also has English collectors from the days when he used to exhibit in London with Fischer Fine Art. Clearly the man has simply damned himself in the eyes of Australia's left-leaning art 'authorities'.

In a sense the large section devoted to Aboriginal art should be the least controversial of the five which make up the total show. Unquestionably Australia's Aboriginal peoples were the first inhabitants of that continent with a history extending back at least 40,000 years.

Inevitably the continent has been settled by others since then – leading initially to conflict and subsequently to a largely misplaced sense of guilt. A great many people have settled in Britain, of course, since the days of its Pictish inhabitants but no-one, so far as I know, has as yet suggested setting up a separate Pictish state even on Black Isle in Scotland, home of Britain's sole Pictish museum.

When I covered the show *Magiciens de la Terre*, which coincided with the celebrations for the 200th anniversary of the French Revolution in Paris, I noted in my review for *The Spectator* how the primitive art of every nation in the world has been diluted and reduced through contact with the West.

Sadly modern Aboriginal art is no exception.

However, one of the greater privileges of my life, during the 17 years I have spent so far in Australia, was to crawl into a cave in the remote sandstone hills of the Cape York Peninsula and see drawings unquestionably made at least 8,000 years ago because that was when one of the creatures depicted – a giant wombat – became extinct. Closely interwoven with such images were those dating from as recently as 150 years ago, at the time of the Palmer River gold rush, which featured mounted native police. Amazingly the style of the drawings remained wonderfully consistent over this entire period.

Nobody at all lives in that immediate area today but it is interesting to reflect, in passing, that Western art since the 1860s has witnessed the passage of up to 100 identifiable art movements.

Might there be something a little bit wrong with us in the West?

In marked contrast to the foregoing, one of the earliest professional trips I made in Australia was to Darwin to cover the prestigious and very handy awards for the latest in Aboriginal art which are held there each year. To my slight surprise, however, a number of the participants looked no more Aboriginal than I did. One at least had bright blue eyes, pale skin and crinkly ginger hair.

When I moved to mention the latter fact in my review of the proceedings my then editor was very quick to dissuade me. I ought to be grateful to her because recently a very well known Australian journalist fell very foul indeed of current, politically correct 'race' legislation for making broadly similar comments.

In post-modern Australia the condition of Aboriginality – which can attract all sorts of rather useful financial benefits – can apparently be a state of mind hardly less than one of genetics, appearance or skin colour.

The Aboriginal art in AUSTRALIA is generally authentic and fascinating and I make my previous comments here largely to illustrate how much Australia is changing these days. Post-modern Australia is certainly no longer a land typified by tough, laconic, hard-drinking cattle drovers – even if it ever was.

Today it is more likely to be a land full of subtle, politically correct pitfalls for the unwary. Post-modern Australia is certainly not quite as simple as it seems but perhaps the recent change of government there will belatedly herald in rather more sensible and constructive times for its citizens – who by now also include me.

The Jackdaw UK, November/December 2013

4

BREXIT STAGE RIGHT

In recent editions of *Annals* I attempted to provide an insight into some of the major reasons why the Western world we inhabit today seems so utterly different in its fundamental nature from the Western world of fifty years ago.

To those who are too young to have known the latter in person, the most likely explanation for this must surely be that our world – together with those of us who now inhabit it – has 'progressed' very rapidly in technological and other ways since those distant-seeming days.

For instance, half a century ago, mobile phones, laptops and internet banking, say, were entirely unknown to us – but then so also was the widespread use of the highly dangerous drug 'ice'. Does that use of 'ice' and other drugs therefore represent some distinctively different but alternative kind of human 'progress'? Quite obviously there are some very major minuses as well as pluses among the umpteen ways in which Western society has changed. In other words change in itself has never been any guarantee of anything for it is every bit as likely to be for the worse as for the better.

In my particular case one of the stranger memories I retain is of being shown a very early form of computer in England all of 45 years ago. The latter consisted of a number of grey metal boxes some of which were almost two metres in height. The American salesman who showed me these, who was himself similarly tall and grey-looking, informed me proudly that what I was looking at 'would do away with the need for ninety secretaries'. What effect the absence of the latter might have on our future employment market was probably beyond that salesman's ability to imagine.

Quite certainly ninety possibly vivacious secretaries seemed to me at that time to possess a bit more potential charm than a collection of huge, singularly inhumane metal boxes but I suspect such a sentiment would simply have struck the salesman proudly showing me this novel invention as culpably 'reactionary' and 'unprogressive'.

I preface my thoughts about the recent departure of Britain from the European Union in the foregoing slightly unusual fashion simply to emphasise how very different the world seemed at the time when Britain joined what was at that time called the European Economic Community back in 1973.

The most dogged former opponent of Britain's entry, eminent French statesman Charles de Gaulle had died slightly more than two years earlier in November 1970 and the door thus suddenly became open to Britain's somewhat belated entry.

Initially Britain's desire to sign up was surely driven more by economic considerations rather than by any sudden discovery of a more 'continental' frame of mind.

Britain had 'recovered after the Second World War much more slowly than either France or Germany which were the dominant members of the EEC from that community's outset, prompting the very common remark in Britain that 'although we won the war we seem to have lost the peace'.

It is extremely easy to forget now that Charles de Gaulle and the German chancellor Konrad Adenauer were closely united not just via their Catholic faith and belief in the vital importance of the family but also by a basic distrust of Britain and of that nation's longer-term motives. Was it just possible that Britain might do some kind of a deal behind their backs with the Soviet Union or – much more probably – succumb totally at some future time to American political, military and economic influences?

Adenauer himself saw the family – as opposed to the political party or some form or other of ideological program – not just as the basic building block of post-war German reconstruction but also as an essential bulwark against the ever-present threat of totalitarian political systems whether from the political Left or the Right. In short for him, at least, *Christian ethics were seen as the essential future basis of German communal life.*

The founding members of the EEC which signed the Treaty of Rome in 1957 were France, Germany, Italy, Belgium, Holland and Luxembourg. When her application to join was initially rejected Britain joined the EFTA instead – the European Free Trade Association – which was then composed of Sweden, Norway, Denmark, Switzerland, Austria and Portugal.

I mention these background details here in the belief that they were probably totally unknown to most of the young British people who were among the most angered by their country's decision to quit the European Union. Some of those have even suggested that the generally older and less educated folk who voted for Brexit ought to have been denied any right to vote and that a second referendum should have been called immediately simply because of the unsatisfactory nature – to their eyes – of the first. Presumably the principles of democracy did not feature highly in those young people's somewhat curious grasp of history.

In the many recent accounts I have read about so-called Brexit I have seen no mention whatsoever of Adenauer's firm belief in the importance of Christian ethics as an absolutely vital future factor within the realms of national and international politics. Indeed if Christianity is no longer deemed to play any particularly important role in our contemporary notions of virtue and of what might be best for humanity at large where precisely should we turn now to find an alternative ethical system of similar completeness?

While pre-Christians in the Old Testament were encouraged to live by the light of ten commandments brought down to them from the mountain, the European Commission in Brussels has shown itself entirely capable now of issuing that number of commandments in a single week.

Non-stop law-making has indeed been a very prominent feature of the EU.

However, as the stalwart journalist Peter Oborne remarked very pointedly in Britain's *The Daily Telegraph* (14.11.2013): "In recent years Europe has fallen under the control of a new ruling class that has obtained powers it has no democratic right to exercise...Highly susceptible to lobby groups and large corporations, it is now out of the reach to political parties and national politicians. This is far more dangerous than has yet been realised. Again and again national leaders have found themselves accountable for decisions they haven't made and can't alter".

If the whole great European enterprise had been limited largely to trade, I believe it would have been infinitely less objectionable to many people in Britain or in other countries which seem hardly less anxious now than Britain to leave the EU.

What remains, in fact, is a system of European government with unpleasantly totalitarian overtones.

Today a single European government and currency, tomorrow some secretly related single system of government perhaps for some other unfortunate section of the globe?

The ambitions of Europe's unelected elite are at least as remarkable as their frequent absence of sense – or of their terrifying inability to foresee inevitable consequences of their actions.

What I am suggesting is that political, social, moral and economic orthodoxies exist in the present day world whose origins are often deeply mysterious and difficult to trace yet which must, of course, have originated somewhere. Do these stem perhaps from pressure groups which are financed by ultra-rich corporations or even by singularly wealthy individuals? I am very far from a conspiracy theorist yet have certain knowledge of some very strange organisations indeed which we are never likely to encounter knowingly in the course of our everyday lives yet whose international influence can nevertheless be profound.

In Britain, lack of control of immigration was surely the most important issue at stake in relation to Brexit – in England especially because that is where almost all new arrivals wish to head. In any one year, half a million new long-term immigrants were likely to arrive and Britain has by now already become the most densely populated country in Europe. In traditionally poor areas unskilled immigrants compete for jobs with the existing unskilled inhabitants so that the adverse effects of such immigration are by no means evenly shared throughout the country. It is in this area especially that one of the EU's founding principles – the free movement of labour – is most likely to be punitive to any indigenous workforce.

The Britain in which I grew up was affected endlessly – and extremely tediously – by industrial action which seriously curtailed the nation's potential rendering it much less competitive in relation to what was already an ever-expanding European industrial performance. Indeed, was knowledge of the sad inadequacy of our own national performance one of the major incentives which threw Britain into the arms of Europe in the first place?

I have mentioned the renewal of Christian faith foreseen by Adenauer and de Gaulle as a most vital factor in Europe's potential for post-war recovery.

Yet moral notions pursued by the EU in recent times have so often been in direct conflict with basic Christian notions of morality that at some stage some fundamental change of ethical allegiance clearly took place within the EU's corridors of power. So-called Human Rights and indeed a European Court of Human Rights have by now entirely entrenched such a change of allegiance. No doubt that is merely one aspect of a 'post-modern' change of emphasis which encompasses all the 'revolutionary' changes which have – for good or ill – been inflicted on Western society at large.

Having never experienced anything else at home, at school or at university many younger people now believe such changes embrace all the necessary components of a social 'morality' which cannot possibly be disputed: political correctness, gender fluidity, global warming, multiculturalism, feminism, abortion on demand and all the other familiar changes brought about basically by the cultural revolutions of the Sixties.

Indeed, one wonders whether some of the more senior figures of the European Commission were former students themselves from the Sorbonne who barricaded the streets of Paris in 1968?

Their apparent foe in those days was 'bourgeois' or traditional France and their instant resort to urban guerilla warfare was, at the time, considered a 'dream tactic' by the Trotskyists of the New Left.

However, at that point 'bourgeois' France belatedly woke up and supporters of de Gaulle also took to the streets of Paris – a million marching under the Cross of Lorraine. The latter people had, of course, known the dire effects of national surrender and of the reign of the Gestapo – but had also lived on ultimately to witness 'liberation'. They were thus none too keen on any recurrence of totalitarian tyranny – however local its source.

When the time came, those privileged children who knew only the supposed inadequacies of a 'bourgeois' state – which they imagined they wished to destroy – belatedly discovered they had nothing much of substance to offer in its place.

'Revolution' is a word which has had much too long a history of popularity in one of the more beautiful lands of our planet. France, accordingly, will always bear the deep scars of its history.

The power-hungry seldom lose their thirst for power even when showing little idea of how to use such power constructively. The EU overstepped basic human commonsense all too frequently until one of its component nations finally rebelled and exited. Much too long ago, the EU ceased to constitute some kind of gentlemanly agreement for mutual advantage and became instead a virtual dictatorship which had little apparent time for national or cultural sensitivities.

For example, nations should never be obliged to admit immigrants who have not the slightest intention of integrating or of respecting the cultures of the countries kind enough to be their hosts. The Europe from which Britain has just exited has by now reached a stage of chaos from which – in its present form – it seems sadly unlikely to emerge.

The long-established academic, artistic and religious traditions which underwrote what we formerly thought of as Europe were utterly priceless and set standards of culture which may never be surpassed.

Not the kind of heritage, in my view, to put into the hands of people so clearly unfitted for the task.

Annals, August 2016

5

THE LONG MARCH REVISITED (PART ONE)

To anyone who has ever been involved in what are known as 'the culture wars' the expression 'the long march' will be thoroughly familiar whereas to almost anyone else it is probably more or less meaningless. Yet in most Western countries, at least, the expression is full of implications which radically affect almost all of our lives.

Back at the turn of the present century, eminent American author and critic Roger Kimball produced a book actually called *The Long March* (Encounter Books 2000) which I reviewed not long after its publication for *The Courier Mail* in Brisbane.

In a recent discussion with the editor of *Annals* I asked him how many readers he thought would be familiar with that book or even with the expression itself. It is as a direct consequence of our talk that I now re-open a subject which continues to hit squarely at the very heart of Western society.

Before discussing the expression further I probably need to give it an approximate date and context – yet before doing even that I am forced to admit that great numbers of Australians exist now who probably believe that any decade which preceded the Sixties merely represents some form of largely irrelevant pre-history. To reinforce that view the vast changes which that decade brought about are also seldom ever questioned now let alone reversed.

Let me therefore begin by directly quoting Kimball himself in one of the many memorable paragraphs from his book: "The Age of Aquarius did not end when the last electric guitar was unplugged at

Woodstock. The 1960s continue to reverberate in our national life today. That decade transformed high culture as well as everyday life in terms of our attitudes toward self and country, sex and drugs, and manners and morality".

So how precisely did the so-called 'long march' occur and what is the precise origin of the expression itself?

In the late 1960s and early 1970s, after immature fantasies of a full-scale political revolution which was aimed to take place in 1968 had very sensibly faded, leading student radicals of that era in France and elsewhere urged their followers to commence instead what they called 'the long march through the institutions'.

Radical German-born philosopher Herbert Marcuse described that particular approach as working *within* institutions while working simultaneously *against* them. The assault, in short, was to be concentrated on the 'soft underbelly' of Western civil life: the arts, education, religion, the law and family life, for instance, where all too few, to their undying shame, could be guaranteed to stand up for the traditional values and virtues of Western civilisation itself in the face of the largely empty, progressivist verbiage peddled – as so often in history – by self-styled political revolutionaries.

Yet as Kimball has remarked: "If you want to see how well the radicals' strategy has succeeded you need look no further now than your local museum, your children's school, your local church (if you still go to church) or your workplace".

Unlike most of my younger co-citizens, however, I can personally remember the decade and a half which preceded the late Sixties not just well but especially vividly. Almost certainly that was because those years had an enhanced sense of reality about them which was surely a legacy of the recently ended Second World War.

In short a great many people in Britain, at least, were profoundly grateful simply to be alive. Evident public respect also still existed for such qualities as honesty, decency, stoicism and neighbourliness as well as for such traditionally martial virtues as bravery in battle. I completed my own two years of compulsory military service during those years and also fulfilled my lifelong ambition to begin a career as an artist just weeks before the much-vaunted Sixties actually began.

Most of the established artists I first met in Cornwall had seen service during the Second World War. A certain degree of hedonism was certainly in the air but in a number of cases that merely represented a kind of pent-up relief after release from capture and years of war-time imprisonment. One artist I met had been taught to paint by another in a prisoner-of-war camp using the oil from cans of sardines furnished kindly by the Red Cross. The dedication of such artists to their calling also lacked the kind of infantile self-righteousness which attended the beginnings of so-called conceptual art some ten years later and of the unruly ideological alliance of Marx and Freud – plus drugs and self-indulgence – which characterised so much art of all kinds during the Sixties.

Somewhere, almost buried by now in public awareness, a belief exists nonetheless that the Sixties heralded in a more enlightened and 'progressive' era in our human consciousness. This somewhat hazy, superficial and largely uninformed view is especially prevalent, in fact, in Australia. Yet the moment we even begin to struggle with some of the more insoluble-seeming problems of life at this moment – such as certain horrific recent consequences of so-called 'multiculturalism' – we also tend to overlook or conveniently forget the basic origin of all such highly dogmatic social ideologies.

At the very beginning of the 1970s a friend of mine went back to university as a mature student with a view to retraining as a lawyer. Simply because we shared a rented house at the time I thus received daily reports of the ways in which feminism and political correctness, for example, were transforming the campus even at that distant time at a conventional-seeming English university. At first some of the novel creeds, at least, seemed to us like very poor jokes indeed yet the real laugh was destined to be on the British public at large when such dogmas shortly became widely enforced as social imperatives.

You may well wonder why such seemingly irreversible social changes happened so quicky and apparently so easily.

Were we all asleep at the wheel perhaps?

The basic message promoted by radical lecturers at that time as well as by their students was that up until very recently 'society' had been doing more or less everything completely wrong.

That was, in a sense, simply a judgement of inexperienced youth about a civilisation of which it had hardly been a significant part. Yet, in a sense, what was happening in previously civilised Western countries could be said to have been merely a very mild echo of the horrors of another 'cultural revolution' which had taken place half a decade earlier in China and of the unleashing of the juvenile Red Guards who were similarly anxious to destroy all vestiges of a major civilisation of which they also had minimal knowledge or understanding.

In the West, China's cultural revolution was widely misrepresented at the time as being a revolt *of* intellectuals when, in fact, it was the exact opposite. What it represented, tragically, was a revolution of illiterates and semi-literates *against* intellectuals and probably had more in common with notorious events in pre-war Nazi Germany – recall the similarly destructive activities of Ernst Roehm's brownshirts – than anything of even the remotest potential for human benefit.

But mass vandalism, of course, is sadly attractive to certain types of radical academic – a species destined to be encountered increasingly often in Europe and North America in the decades which followed the Sixties.

The 'cultural revolution' which featured the Red Guards has subsequently been characterised by distinguished English historian Paul Johnson as "the greatest witch-hunt in history which made the Zhdanov purges in post-war Russia seem almost trivial". Roger Kimball and English philosopher Roger Scruton aside, Paul Johnson has been one of the more damning critics of the long-term social, religious and cultural consequences of the Sixties. In an article in a recent issue of *Annals* I quote Roger Scruton who relates some of the extremely adverse consequences for his academic and writing career of taking a similar stand.

The hegemony exercised by political pseudo-revolutionaries – also known by the preferred more recent term as neo-Marxists – in Western academic and cultural life remains an ongoing disfigurement of almost all Western democratic societies today but also argues the almost total success of 'the long march' the existence of which is by now approaching its full half century.

Indeed if we care to cast our minds back exactly half a century we return to the days when Mao Tse-tung – who remains possibly the greatest monster in the whole of human history – still drew widespread praise in the West. Indeed in a recently published book *The Cultural Revolution: A People's History, 1962-1976* (Bloomsbury) Frank Dikotter relates tales so harrowing of mass extermination and even cannabilism as to defy human belief yet much of that book is based on the study of hitherto unexamined archives by one of the world's leading authorities on 20th century China. Mr. Dikotter is professor of humanities at the University of Hong Kong and is the author already of many studies on China.

Mao's undoubted aim was to destroy Chinese history and culture in a manner which could never be repaired and we should perhaps acknowledge now the extent to which cultural revolutionaries in the West shared much the same aim in relation to our own priceless, formerly largely Christian way of life.

Was there genuinely so little that deserved saving from the incomparable history of Western writers, poets, painters, sculptors, composers, playwrights, architects and actors to say nothing of religious mystics, major scholars, lawyers and historians?

In days when I had the good fortune or otherwise to be a regular visiting lecturer at English art schools during the pinnacle of the post-modernist phase the phrase I learned to dread most was one uttered regularly then by female students: "my artwork challenges the existing patriarchal paradigm".

Very sadly this was often said by a student who could barely grasp which end of a pencil to use.

Post-modernist dogma which came to power within British tertiary education on the back of the so-called culture wars had – and still has – a great deal to answer for in its deliberate demolition of a much more genuine and deserving culture.

I am tempted at times to describe the post-modernist era as a unique one which has attempted to elevate idiocy to the status of orthodoxy. Fifty years ago the so-called 'Safe Schools Program' which has been inflicted recently on Victorian Schools would have been inconceivable but here we encounter a phenomenon with which I have long been familiar.

All one basically needs to do is describe any ill-judged initiative as 'progress' for far too many otherwise sensible thinkers to flee the field. We live in a time, in fact, when mere rhetoric is all too inclined to rule the roost whereas in my own former discipline of the visual arts all rhetorical claims were at least subject to the need to provide visual evidence. Take a look at what the late 17th century produced, in short, in terms of painting and then compare that if you will with supposedly major work from the late 20th century.

Progress or regress?

The eyes are all that is basically needed to provide a favourable or unfavourable verdict.

At especially irreverent moments I picture two Aussie soldiers up to their ears in mud in a wartime foxhole.

"What particular major causes do you feel you are fighting for mate?" one asks the other.

"Put me down for gender fluidity" the other one replies.

What post-modernism has achieved across the board is for society to part company increasingly with any form of tangible reality and even with the absolutely fundamental notion of the existence of singular truth.

Virtually all police work and investigative journalism presupposes that the latter exists but do not even dare to suggest such an idea within the walls of any post-modernist academic institution.

The proverbial long march has by now taken us all about as far as it can go in a largely worthless and anti-social direction.

Has the time come finally perhaps for us all to cry 'halt' and to begin a long march back again to some place where – as God's creatures – we much more truly belong?

Annals, June 2016

6

THE LONG MARCH
REVISITED (PART TWO)

In the last edition of *Annals* I touched upon a vast but endlessly relevant subject: in short the manner in which Sixties ideologies have effectively transformed Western society not always – but very much too often – for the worse.

In doing so I quoted from Roger Kimball's *The Long March* (Encounter Books 2000) and make no apology for doing so now again: "For over two hundred years, the Left has had an effective but unearned monopoly on the rhetoric of virtue. *The Long March* scrutinizes that unearned monopoly and attempts to expose the spuriousness of radical claims to liberation. As with most revolutions, the counterculture's call for total freedom quickly turned into a demand for total control. The phenomenon of 'political correctness' with its speech codes and other efforts to enforce ideological conformity was one predictable result of this transformation."

We surely know only too well what 'political correctness' is but what precisely does Kimball mean here by "the rhetoric of virtue"?

Very early in my own writing career I became acutely aware of the grossly distorting effect created by rhetorical use of language in the visual arts – hardly less so, in fact, than in politics. Indeed, in the former case such charged use of language substantially underpinned the movements known to us today as 'modernism' and 'post-modernism'.

In fact, by effectively impounding nouns such as progress, evolution, development, advance and (bold) experiment for its own exclusive use so-called modernism not only furthered the causes of frequently feeble and highly confused art but also prolonged its own effective lifespan.

No less to the point any opposition at all to such purely supposed 'progress' and 'evolution' in art could then be characterised as reactionary, conservative, head-in-the-sand, seeking-to-put-the-clock-back and so forth.

What a breathtakingly effective rhetorical trick!

But why did it take so many quite so long to see through this relatively simple piece of verbal deception?

To make matters worse avant-gardism in all of the arts also tried — very successfully in the event — to align its causes rhetorically, at least, with the often huge but *perfectly genuine* advances which were taking place simultaneously in a wide variety of technological fields.

Was there ever a more cleverly conceived rhetorical confidence trick than the above which has been perpetrated on society-at-large?

Should I perhaps mention here that during the heyday of highly 'advanced' modernist musical composition public performances of the aforesaid in Britain could generally be guaranteed only by sandwiching such supposedly ground-breaking music between hefty helpings of baroque or classical music which had been created by composers known to be revered by the public?

In short in order to sell concerts featuring 'advanced' composers such as Berg, Boulez or Birtwistle it was generally necessary to 'top and tail' such public performances with strong helpings of music by the likes of Brahms, Beethoven or Bach.

Was this one of the first pieces of evidence, in fact, of the widely ignored 'general public' effectively fighting back against the entrenched conceits of our cultural controllers?

In short, left to its own devices, 'advanced' atonal music was never successful in attracting viable concert audiences in Britain.

That said I do not for a moment deny that so-called modernism produced its share of interesting and sometimes praiseworthy practitioners across many artistic disciplines yet what should really have been encouraged by our bodies of state patronage all along was resolute individualism rather than conformity to some example or other of extremist avant-garde creed.

What ought to be self-evident here, in fact, is that left to its own devices mere novelty may or may not offer society any guarantee of value in any of the arts – or, for that matter, in any other aspect of our lives.

Indeed, how wonderful it would be if a moratorium could be called now on the endlessly deceptive use of words such as 'progress' and 'progressive' in the world of culture no less than of political life.

What I suggest here is that it does not take any great feat of imagination to realise the disproportionate extent to which rhetorical use of language has by now taken a dangerously coercive role not just in the arts but in virtually every other aspect of recent human existence.

During our current federal election, for example, some matters which are sure to be described glibly as 'progressive' will almost certainly turn out to be regressive or even morally decadent in the long run.

So how precisely did we get ourselves into quite such a rhetorical and moral quagmire in the first place?

Here is Roger Kimball once again in a further quotation from his book: "It has been in the life of art and the life of the mind, however, that the counterculture has had its most devastating effects. To an extent which would have been difficult to imagine thirty years ago, art and education have become handmaidens of political radicalism. Standards in both have plummeted. The art world has more and more jettisoned any concern with beauty and has become a playground for bogus 'transgressive' gestures. Colleges and universities, aping this exhausted radicalism, have given themselves up to an uneasy mixture of politically correct causes and the rebarbative rhetoric of deconstruction, poststructuralism and 'cultural' studies. The story of what has happened to our institutions of high culture since the Sixties is a story of almost uninterrupted degradation and pandering to forces inimical to culture".

When I was a young man in England in the early 1960s, public interest in the visual arts, literature, poetry, theatre, ballet and films could hardly have been more enthusiastic or, in many cases, more uplifting to the human spirit but such is the radical and predictably Left-wing political nature of so much of our culture in Australia today that what is easily the finest intellectual and literary magazine in this country *Quadrant* has just had its modest annual grant cut to zero by the Australia Council after sixty highly distinguished years of publication. Without *Quadrant, The Spectator* and *Annals,* Australia would indeed be almost totally dominated by journals solely promoting the causes of neo-Marxism and the hard Left. The Australia Council which supposedly represents all of us has no business whatsoever to act in this way.

So why does the Australia Council, as a public body, throw in its lot so eagerly with the forces of political radicalism?

All I need to do here perhaps is refer once more to the quote from Roger Kimball with which I began this article: "For over two hundred years, the Left has had an effective but unearned monopoly on the rhetoric of virtue".

What I therefore sense is that some particular set of public servants employed by the Australia Council is anxious to damage the publication of *Quadrant* simply because that magazine has the courage to publish a wide range of liberal, conservative and other 'alternative' opinions.

Occasionally, I admit, I find myself forgetting that Australia is still supposedly a democracy.

Indeed, readers with more experience than I of living here may be kind enough to remind me of what percentage of the total poll the CPA – the Communist Party of Australia – has ever achieved in any federal election here?

If national elections in Britain are any guide to such matters two per cent of the total vote would be the highest figure I could possibly imagine. Why then does the influence of the radical far Left remain so absolutely ubiquitous in Australia especially in our national seats of culture?

I do not believe for a moment that that is what our general populace wants.

However, 'the long march through the institutions' conceived fifty or more years ago as an attack on the soft underbelly of Western civil life – the arts, education, publishing, religion, the law and family life – could by now be said to have been almost totally successful in excluding the opinion of the general public more or less completely from any discussion.

But why need any of us put up with such a situation indefinitely?

As just one consequence of political narrowmindedness the arts in Australia are seriously retarded and provincialised largely through the overt left-wing politicisation of our 'public funding' bodies.

Indeed, those many 'public' intellectuals here who imagine themselves to be neo-Marxists must presumably be quite comfortable with the history of communism which witnessed the deaths during the twentieth century alone of some 100 million of *its own peoples.*

During my compulsory service the military body with which I served was separated from the Russian forces which occupied the adjacent section of Northern Germany by just a few hundred metres of snow and ice.

If conflict had occurred the young Soviet soldiers and the men from the unit to which I was attached were required to eliminate each other as quickly and efficiently as possible but I must confess here to having felt rather less emnity to the young servicemen of that former 'enemy' side than I do to all the would-be intellectuals from Western countries who have consistently betrayed Western values and ideals both before and after the distant days of the Cold War.

The stated aim of the latter has been to erode Western, and more specifically Christian society *from within* by all means possible until it collapses finally of its own accord... and is then replaced by 'something or other' – but what exactly will that 'something or other' be?

What about the 'gender fluid' fantasy world envisaged by Roz

Ward and the Safe Schools Program which she co-promotes?

So far as I can ascertain, Ms Ward read 'gender studies' at Sussex University in England and since the information imparted on that course may possibly represent almost all of what she knows it is perhaps understandable that she should try to pass that course's somewhat unusual findings on to the Australian nation at large. But are we – or our children – quite ready yet for its supposedly 'advanced' – and entirely unbelievable – notions?

In England, some while ago, it was common knowledge that ever-increasing numbers of so-called 'mickey mouse' degrees existed at British universities which helped keep in check unemployment figures among the young.

In my own days of working in England 'environmental studies' at Birmingham University was possibly the most notorious of such degrees and could apparently be accessed then by applicants with very low grades indeed.

In my recent review of a book by English philosopher Roger Scruton I repeated his complaint about the extreme political bias of nearly all courses in the arts and humanities in present-day Western universities. In a sense, the history of the so-called 'long march' and the history of the antinomian sentiment of the Sixties provides a total explanation of such bias.

When I was growing up in England, the defection to the Soviet Union by members of the British Intelligence Services such as Burgess, McLean and Philby still made national and international headlines and all were described unhesitatingly at the time as 'traitors' to Western causes. Quite certainly the upholding of Christian civilisation in the face of atheistic totalitarian empires – such as the former USSR – would still have been considered precisely such a cause.

Now, however, we are rendered so mindless through incessant brainwashing by our largely compliant media as to accept the erosion from within of almost all that is historically priceless in Western civilisation.

Indeed, we very generally treat such erosion now as an inescapable

– and almost minor fact – of our contemporary existences. Decades ago now, American Judge Robert Bork famously described Western society as "slouching towards Gomorrah".

The actual phrase "the long march through the institutions" is often attributed to the Italian Marxist philosopher Antonio Gramsci but was actually the brainchild of German New Leftist Rudi Dutschke.

What 'the long march' has attempted is not just the overthrow of Western culture in a narrow sense but a rewriting of the moral and civil codes which underwrite the entire God-inspired history of Western civilisation.

Is that really what we want?

Annals, July 2016

_7_

TBILISI DOES IT

'I'd rather have a bottle in front o' me than a frontal lobotomy', so, reputedly, said the noted imbiber and entertainer W.C.Fields. In Moscow, in the almost certain absence of a bottle, due to the heavy-handed nature of the current Soviet campaign against drunkenness, even the second alternative makes increasing sense to help overcome the frustrations encountered when trying to do anything other than remain completely inert.

In Moscow activity of any kind brings one into inevitable contact with the subtle blend of obstructiveness, slowness and ingrained inefficiency unique to Russian life. Little doubt we are spoiled in the West by such luxuries as telephone systems that work, baths with plugs or restaurants that serve. Nor should serious students of Kafka omit the mind-chilling experience of the Rossya Hotel. Opened in 1966 and with 3,000 rooms, it is not only the world's largest hotel but easily the most confusing to try to traverse.

The decision of AICA, the International Association of Art Critics, to hold its annual conference in Tbilisi was a bold one. However, after two days in Moscow. Tbilisi seems notably warm and friendly. Traditionally there is little love lost between Georgians, whose capital this is, and Muscovites. Tbilisi is bounded on three sides by mountains, lying to the South of the steepling peaks of the Greater Caucasus, between the Black Sea and the Caspian.

An industrialised city has sprung up amid a basic, agricultural landscape from Asia Minor. For this reason fresh fruit, vegetables and wine, unseen in Moscow, are readily available here, though regrettably fax and telex machines are not. A BBC unit trying to work here has found the average time to reach London by telephone is at least two hours. When I managed to get connected in just 20 minutes, at one a.m. admittedly, to explain problems I might find in trying to get this copy in, I had possibly set a new record. In the meantime two French delegates had still to speak to Paris after three days of trying.

Formalities aside, the 23rd Congress of AICA got under way appropriately with a stirring paper read by a young Russian art critic Alexander Yakimovich. Some of the old guard expressed incredulity that he had been allowed to speak at all. It was easy to see why. His passionate thesis is that contemporary art in the Soviet Union remains in a 'post-catastrophic' stage today, implying a post-traumatic psychology. The trauma relates to a period when "no man, no artist, no thinker, no scientist in the Soviet Union could feel safe…high intellect, artistic talent, positive social activity or true moral standards were mortally dangerous for their bearers…the catastrophic aspects of Soviet totalitarianism exceeded known historical calamities by the very aspect which differentiates Dante's Hell from Purgatory: no hope is left".

These are terrible words indeed, describing terrible and none-too-distant experiences. Wounds will not heal quickly in Russia nor, in a sense, should they.

The Western capitalism against which Soviet leaders formerly inveighed is an economic and social, not an ethical system. As an economic system it works better than communism – but that is not difficult since communism does not work at all. However, what any system needs today, for any lasting degree of success, is some ethical umbrella. Economic and social systems depend ultimately on human good will; to encourage or provide moral ideologies which promote the latter is a vital intellectual priority.

However, after Yakimovich's stirring words, the concerns expressed in papers given by most Western critics were, in the main, academic, semantic or solipsist. To be in Russia at this time is to be conscious of experiencing a moment of extraordinary or even unique historical potential.

Art and criticism have a part to play by showing fresh concern for relevance, honesty and openness. Sadly, many of the 20-odd speakers mumbled their way through papers the meaning of which would be none too easy to grasp even in their original language. One German delivered his paper in such a mangling of English that it defeated even the best efforts of our multilingual translators. Delegates could choose any tongue for their delivery and while a Norwegian delegate spoke clearly in French others chose tongues over which their command was far from perfect. I am glad to say the British speakers, Sara Wilson, Brandon Taylor, Keith Patrick and Malcolm Carr were clear and concise and even attempted humour.

For me. other than Yakimovich's, the outstanding paper of the conference was that of Hans-Jorg Heusser, director of the Swiss Institute for Art Research in Zurich. His concerns for historical truth in art and linguistic clarity were laudable. The particular pleasure of Heusser's paper was that it echoed many of the concerns expressed in this column, though more eloquently perhaps. The forming of professional friendships across the barriers of nation justifies such conferences, however ponderous their nature.

Our Georgian hosts are sharp-nosed, dark-skinned and fierce of mien. During their many occasions of most lavish and generous hospitality some determined to claim me as a natural Georgian. Were I to assume their diet of sweet, spicy food, flavoured by a relative of coriander, or violent alcohol, my shape might also come close to the role-model offered by the highly successful sculptor Mirab Berdzanishvil. His monumental work embodies a violent, almost theatrical baroque; it is easy to imagine that a land of warriors would find his battle memorials hugely moving. Far odder, to Western eyes, was the work of Zurab Tserteli, who is even more phenomenally successful. Both sculptors live and entertain like mediaeval princes in a land of supposed socialist equality.

The kiosk of my would-be Westernised hotel offers an ageing copy of the *Morning Star* as its sole English-language newspaper. I see this as a symbolic relic of fatuous and murderous social experiment.

In the streets outside, stone-age taxis driven by would-be Grand Prix drivers hurtle straight at anyone intrepid enough to hail them. To my terror, I must secure one of these now to attend the closing moments of the Congress.

The Spectator UK, 30 September 1989

8

PETNAJST-TRIDESET
(15-30)

At the risk of straining the credulity of readers and the patience of my editor, this week finds me in Rogaska Slatina playing in the 16[th]world tennis championships for professional journalists.

If you cannot locate this venue immediately either in your mind or on a map, it lies in Slovenia not far from the border with Croatia. The peace and serenity of early September in this region almost defies description. Of course, much the same applies to what people are doing to each other somewhat further to the South in former Yugoslavia.

Slovenia is a country of roughly the same size as Wales but with a population of just two million. It boasts regions and towns of outstanding and even unique beauty – the limestone Karst, for instance. The early September weather approaches perfection and everywhere there is evidence of mellow fruitfulness: vines, pumpkins, apples, hops.

The tournament is played on continental clay courts which tend to upset the ability to time the ball even of good players from elsewhere. I do not expect the tennis to make major inroads into time set aside for reflection. That said, it is the belief of some competitors that the age and levels of articulacy of certain former winners of this tournament suggested they delivered papers rather than wrote for them.

As you would imagine, many of the assembled journalists write or broadcast about sport. I suspect I may be the only art critic present. Although my surname is one of the shorter, it seems to provide peculiar difficulties of spelling and pronunciation for the organisers; this may be because the letters c,j,k and z do not feature in it either prominently or in sequence.

With some time on my hands I have asked myself not for the first time why, as a person of strong artistic inclination, I have found such keen pleasure all my life in playing sport. As I have grown older the answer has become clearer: in marked contrast to the world of contemporary art in which I work, most of the sports I have played have clear-cut rules. Thus tennis provides a searching test of technique and character as well as athleticism. But how big a role do the two former aspects play today in the making of art? In spite of the dissent of a few, the shallow, dishonest and modish has been praised so frequently in contemporary art that many think no rules of any kind can be applied any longer.

Most young artists with whom I speak seem to believe this by now and have become cynical and disillusioned in consequence. They think that success in art is simply a lottery and so lose the incentive to develop and hone accepted skills. By contrast, the general clarity of rules in sport promotes mutual respect – among amateur players at least. Although some sharp practice exists, results in sport generally promote a feeling that justice is done. What a difference from the art world!

Yet art, too, could be much more reassuring to a human race currently in greater need of confirmation than destruction of values. In the village of Olimje near the town of Atomske Toplice which, like Rogaska, is a spa, the carved and gilded wooden figures behind the altar in a painted, baroque church reveal a level of craftsmanship and artistry all but extinct in the present-day world. Yet they were the work not of artists but of monks. Their subjects concern what were thought of once as the great verities of human existence which, like the great truths of art, have been submerged for a long time now under seas of questioning. Indeed, almost every worthwhile thing in art is queried or deconstructed today, yet little or nothing is offered by way of answers.

When we look at the European art of previous centuries, clear hierarchies have been established based on the skill, imagination and talent of artists. Such hierarchies did not happen by accident. In days gone by artists learned their skills from established practitioners – the tennis coaches of art – and practised daily in studios rather than out on the courts. Sometimes those of less obvious or flamboyant skills triumphed in the end through sheer application – just as in tennis, in fact.

The setting of personal targets is one of the pleasures of sport. Those like me who are not content to lose can work out for themselves or be shown by others how to improve their performance. The saddest aspect for me of visiting studio complexes of young artists is that none seem to have the slightest idea what to do now or how to improve their work in the future. Would adding bits of old wallpaper to their latest productions unlock the door to fame and fortune? With the silliness of current critical criteria it very well might.

In the meantime, nearly every such young artist I see is hopelessly adrift, ill advised, appallingly taught, sold out by the rottenness of our fashionable system. Even when they seem supportive, modish critics and curators are often the undoing of such artists by persuading them to base a whole lifetime's activity on the flimsiest and most transient of foundations. Many artists I see bemoan how little the unjust world of capitalism is doing for them, style themselves as Marxists and delude themselves meanwhile that their art deals in startling realities.

At Rogaska, a senior, well-qualified and extremely charming Hungarian journalist I had played against told me he earned the equivalent of just 300 pounds sterling per month. He was five when the last world war ended and he explained with sadness but no self-pity how the best years of his life had been taken away from him by living under the dead hand of communism.

To meet such a person is a privilege, but the time has come now and I must return to the utter anarchy and unreality of the world of living art in the West.

The Spectator UK, 10 September 1993

9

PAYING FOR
VAN GOGH'S EAR

'The best treatment for jet lag,' a smart (art) dealer counsels me, 'is a line of coke'. We are in New York, city of frenzied energy, at a party given by a famous firm of fine art auctioneers and I am feeling somewhat less than fresh off the plane.

This is a city wherein to feel tired, let alone weak or poor, is really not acceptable. So shunning any pathetic instincts for survival, I find myself still to be more or less upright at a night-club several hours later. When I leave, scores of bright young men and girls are dancing what little remains of the night away. Do none have jobs to cope with later in the morning?

When writing more usually from the other side of the Atlantic, the influence of New York on our perception of art in Britain often strikes me as of questionable benefit. When the United States decided to steamroller tired old European culture in the late Fifties, New York supplied the economic clout and intellectual energy to make an excellent job of the operation. If the aim had been to make us Europeans perceive ourselves as artistically provincial, the stratagem was at least temporarily successful. For a long time the stars of art and of the museum hierarchy in Britain dwelt lovingly upon the greater opportunities and 'buzziness' of American culture.

Hockney was merely one of our *Wunderkinder* who, but for a tightening of immigration laws, might have turned a trickle of art migrants into a stampede.

Fame and fortune seemed there to be grabbed by those sufficiently fast on their feet. Yet might there not be some unseen or unacceptable reckoning to come one day from this contract with Mammon? Kindness and hospitality notwithstanding, my experience of New York this week makes me feel there may be something unseen but sinister eating away at the inside of the artistic Apple.

Money is certainly not the ostensible problem. At Sotheby's sale mainly of Impressionist and Post-Impressionist paintings which I attended here on 9 May, virtually every individual sales record was broken save that of the highest price for a single work. Over $204 million was realized, a figure approaching double the previous highest total reached last month at Sotheby's London. At $47.9 million, Picasso's early self-portrait became the second highest-priced work ever, after van Gogh's 'Irises'. In the words of the auctioneer, as prices leapt up in increments of $2 million, "*This* is what it's all about".

In the euphoria of the moment, few in the audience would have dreamt of disabusing him. Perhaps most knew no better, nor yet anything of the lives of the artists for whose often minor works they were willing to part with so much mazooma.

One does not wish to sound sanctimonious, yet a few reflections on the perils of a money-dominated culture might not be inappropriate, especially in these parts. The values inherent in great art provide us with an alternative to and a refuge from the venal. Indeed, any attempt to reduce art to the level of merchandise is a denial of the uncompromising levels of thought which should go into the making of it. At one time major collectors and dealers still felt deeply for the treasures under their temporary control. Today one suspects these are increasingly becoming seen merely as the ultimate in designer wallpaper. It is a pity that some minor test of art historical knowledge cannot be made as a condition for the ownership of masterpieces. From the appearance and conversations of many present at this week's series of great auctions here I doubt whether too many would pass it.

Last week's sale of Impressionist and modern works at Christie's, New York, broke several records also, and one cannot help thinking that notional catalogue estimates are playing a part in this process, for they have come to be viewed now as accurate indications of value. Bidding was often wildly inconsistent with the merits of individual paintings by the same artist. One of the week's most interesting Pissarros (of Le Havre) fetched far less than lesser-seeming works. The reason? A factory chimney in the background which might remind buyers of the true sources of their wealth.

The virtue of the New York art market lies in its vigour and volume, yet its major vice remains lack of genuine discrimination. One salutes the energy and willingness to spend money on art, yet the good effect of this can be nullified by a fatal lack of the confidence that comes from real knowledge. Thus buyers accept too willingly the opinions of others rather than relying on their own. In terms of contemporary art in New York, one can now propose and sell almost anything providing the price ticket is high enough. Good writing could help counter this tendency and prevent the cynical belief that one can overcome arts current ills simply by throwing more money at them. Contemporary art here is still bedevilled by the notion of paying for van Gogh's ear – feelings of residual guilt about the treatment of major talents in the art-historical past. The latter paralyses present will and turns the condition of contemporary art here into a destructive lottery.

The other day I followed a posse of rich American matrons on their conducted tour of the Whitney Museum of American Art.

'The poin of this picksher' droned the guide in control 'is whether you see the blue infrunner the yeller, or the yeller infrunner the blue'. I wept for the decent folk who accepted this garbled gospel so humbly. The Whitney is host at present to a biennial show of what is supposed to be the best and brightest of the coming generation of American artists. On the evidence of this show, which I will describe in detail next week, the ship of art here is rudderless and sinking. An apocalyptic rainstorm accompanied my visit and, as I emerged into the continuing deluge, a smiling negro was consoling his friend. 'Rain's only water, man', he said.

If only the ills of this city's art climate could be explained so simply.

The Spectator UK, 20 May, 1989

10

DRUGGED BY THE DOLLAR

In New York last week a local radio station reported two cases of householders who had been awakened at night by alarms fitted to their cars. On rushing into the street to investigate, the first had been shot dead on his doorstep while the second was stabbed to death after briefly chasing the would-be thief. These events did not take place in Harlem or the Bronx but in Queens and New Jersey. Asked by the radio interviewer to give his views on the advisability of fitting car alarms, a police spokesman was moved to say: 'If someone wants your car give him the keys'.

Those who suffer a lawless society anywhere merit our sympathy, for nothing provokes despair and cynicism so quickly. In New York the anarchy of the streets extends also, I believe, to the world of contemporary visual arts wherein a parallel sense of debilitation – of an intellectual kind – permeates the structure.

Anyone requiring evidence of this dereliction of values could do no better than visit the current Biennial at the Whitney Museum of American Art at East 75th Street. The show purports to survey the best and brightest of young American painters, sculptors, photographers and video-makers. If this were truly the case, one might be excused for muttering 'God help us', because the powerful influences of American art extend far and wide.

Indeed no sooner are the younger stars of American art established in New York than they are exported eastwards; exhibitions in Britain and West Germany allow apologists for such art to add the epithet 'international' to their burgeoning stardom. The flattering reputations enjoyed in the USA by the likes of Julian Schnabel, Susan Rothenberg,

Jeff Koons or Donald Baechler strike most of us in Britain as deeply mysterious when their works come to be seen here. This may be because our critical and intellectual faculties remain awake and have not succumbed entirely to what an English artist more familiar than I with American culture describes aptly as 'the chloroform of the dollar'. When I talked in America of the urgent need to re-establish more lasting critical values, I was looked on as though visiting from some other galaxy. I feel painters who enter art simply with easy money in view would be more honourably employed in estate agency.

Indeed if art fails to provide some spiritual and aesthetic alternative to the venal and ugly it loses all human, let alone divine justification. One essential test of individual artistic activity, so I believe, is whether the artist would continue with it in the absence of hope of reward. Thus would one rush from one's bed each morning to stencil dozy cartoon ostriches onto sheets of plywood as does Sherrie Levine, or to paint the word 'please' six times in stencilled lettering on five yards of aluminium sheet, as does Christopher Wool? There is scarcely a piece of painting or sculpture at the Whitney which looked as though it would provide the least joy or satisfaction in making, yet prior to this century such intrinsic reward was a feature of the making of virtually all visual art. Needless to say, the Whitney show promotes itself as being part of the vital innovatory 'cutting edge' of contemporary culture. Who or what is being cut has yet to be specified. One might speak of the artists cutting their own throats were it not for the fact that most are undoubtedly prospering. I can but hope they find something satisfying and engaging to do in their leisure hours.

The current Whitney Biennial features almost every available form of visual inanity, ranging from what looks rather like an automatic vending machine – cryptically called 'Tormented Self-Portrait (Susie at Arles)' – via much drab and indifferent geometrical abstraction, to tacky figurines and sheets of rubber stretched between steel rods. All are accompanied by written notes of breathtaking portentousness, as is the exhibition as a whole. So much money sloshes around in the bowl of contemporary art in New York that a painful awareness of this wealth permeates the art on view. Artists who, while lacking discernible talent, become very rich indeed set an unfortunate example. I fear that in an absence of agreed values contemporary art takes on the status of an obscene lottery with artists searching ever more desperately for winning combinations. In New York the market for contemporary art is so huge and insatiable that artists make wilder and wilder guesses in the hope of tapping into the golden vein. Two artists at the Whitney – Cary Smith and Jeff Koons – even rely on a capacity to irritate the onlooker to achieve their ends.

'These colours and their interaction on the picture surface are intended to be an irritant. He (Smith) is attempting to provoke a visual response that approximates to controlled hysteria or nervous apprehension' and 'Slavishy crafted by European artisans, Koons's pieces are overheated, sentimental, vigorously repulsive'. Donald Baechler, another putative star of this show, believes 'the best art is not in museums but on toilet walls'. He paints accordingly.

In spite of the goodwill of thousands of earnest modern art administrators and the expenditure of millions of whatever currency you choose, our age has managed to make itself a benighted artistic era which rivals the most misguided and decadent in human history. Exhibitions such as that at the Whitney point to an urgent need for greater intellectual vigour in everything we do.

Yet as long ago as 1971, Hilton Kramer. the most articulate New York art critic of his day, had already uttered the necessary warning: "For the new academy of innovation, which is what the museum culture of the avant-garde has come to be, is no more able than other academies to encompass the pressures of new experience, it can only satisfy existing taste and minister to empty prejudice...The task of criticism today is, in large part, an archaeological task – the task of digging out a lost civilization from the debris that has swamped and buried it'.

Hand me a shovel, Hilton.

The Spectator UK, 27 May 1989

11

OLYMPIAN REFLECTIONS

What lessons, if any, can we take away from the recently held Olympic Games in London especially, perhaps, in relation to the physical and moral development of today's children?

As Olympic records continued to fall in a wide range of disciplines it was clear that standards of training, coaching, expertise and equipment have all continued to rise and I cannot help reflecting here, at least occasionally, on how inadequate such matters generally were in the days of my own youth.

Thus a fellow pupil at my school who later played in a Rugby Union trial for England trained habitually by running endless miles on hard roads shod in army boots with a haversack full of large stones strapped to his back.

Guts and determination were certainly not lacking in his case even though modern levels of equipment and expertise fairly obviously were.

While the Olympics were taking place – the men's road cycling time trial won by Bradley Wiggins actually passed my front door – I noticed rather a sour on-line commentary from Australia's Channel 9 which hinted darkly that much of Britain's success was confined to 'elitist' sports, for which a horse or somesuch expensive accessory was necessary, and that many of Britain's successful Olympians had also attended private schools. The inference seemed to be that a good deal of Britain's Olympic success had thus been bought rather than earned.

Dare one ask here what the proclaimed role of the government-funded Australian Institute of Sport is if not the development of 'elite' sporting standards?

Dare I also admit here that I attended an English private school as a boarder myself – albeit on a scholarship?

Certainly in my day the overwhelming ethos of such schools was about as different as it could be from that prevalent in most of the state schools of today that I have visited in recent years in England or Australia.

Muscular Christianity – with a strong dash of militarism – would probably be a fair summary of the values promoted formerly at my school.

But then duty, courage, discipline, responsibility and intense competitiveness – academic as well as physical – were certainly core values also in most of Britain's other single-sex, Anglican boarding schools of my day.

In my own case and probably that of most boarders who were similarly removed completely from parental care for 3 months at a time – the length of an English school term – such sons of civilised parents would often compete at sport like savages. Given such an atmosphere you may find it easy to imagine that playing the violin, say – however brilliantly – did not really begin to compare with prowess at rugby, cricket or athletics.

In the famous words attributed rightly or wrongly to the Duke of Wellington: "The battle of Waterloo was won on the playing fields of Eton."

Yet the book which truly made England's major boarding schools famous – or infamous – *Tom Brown's School Days* by Thomas Hughes – was not published until 42 years after that historic battle although the experience on which it was based related largely to the author's own days at Rugby between 1834 and 1842.

Many who have read that book will probably recall the brutalities it describes rather than its strong advocacy of innocence, decency, leadership and compassion. What would probably also surprise many however is how little the basic character of Britain's private boarding schools changed from Tom Brown's school days to my own which coincided roughly with the final, post-war demise of the British Empire.

In a sense, concentration on the forming of stalwart character in such schools – plus an ability to think and act independently – served the former requirements of an overseas empire and those of Britain's armed services extremely well. Indeed, that was once undoubtedly a major part of its purpose.

Channel 9's commentary which hinted that it was simply the superior sporting facilities enjoyed by pupils at privileged private schools that made the difference thus ignored the fundamental role which a highly competitive ethos also plays in that equation. Indeed, in recent times in a great many state schools in England competitiveness at sport was actively discouraged by well-meaning if seriously wrong-minded progressivist teachers. A wish to excel had previously been believed by almost everyone to be a natural human impulse.

Lack of motivation and classroom discipline aside, what other major changes have I noticed in secondary education over the past few decades?

As any significant element of Christian teaching has generally declined – other than in specifically Christian schools – so it has been replaced increasingly by covert or even overt political indoctrination predominantly of a left-wing and politically correct nature.

Indeed a good deal of hypocrisy and double standards seem to be at work here because if the teaching of Christian principles to students from non-Christian backgrounds can be held to be wrong – as well as against the wishes of non-Christian parents – then surely left-wing indoctrination of the children of even mildly conservative parents is at least as indefensible?

Yet because of the political orientations of most members of teaching unions employed in public education that is what is happening today in almost all forms of secondary public schooling throughout the Western world.

In the years after I left school considerable prejudice existed in intellectual circles against the playing of competitive sport to the extent that a young man of my acquaintance who played squash to international standards habitually carried his sports kit in a guitar case.

Now, suddenly, in the days of post-Olympics euphoria everyone in Britain seems to be saying how good sport is for all children and how much such a view ought to be generally encouraged.

The latter is a view with which I certainly concur, yet education of children as a whole has by now lost its way generally and not just in the matter of sport. Thus academic standards have generally been on the decline for years in Britain in spite of the claims habitually made by the teaching unions.

Clearly this latter is a justified source of annoyance to most thinking parents who wish to equip their children as adequately as they can for their futures in adult life.

Here the development of healthy bodies should clearly run parallel to academic development yet today, in most state schools, this still ignores a third element – the development of moral and civic character – which also once formed a vital part of the whole offered by a traditional British private education.

By curious chance the school I attended fell in the political constituency of Sir Winston Churchill who accordingly borrowed our school hall, which boasted the largest available auditorium in the area, at least occasionally for speaking purposes.

In terms of patriotic oratory, I believe Churchill's famous war-time speeches to the House of Commons bear comparison even with Shakespeare's finest – e.g the St. Crispian's Day speech from Henry V.

Yet how many could be relied upon to rise without question today to the sentiment expressed by Churchill in June 1940 to the British people: "Let us brace ourselves to our duty, and so bear ourselves that, if the British Empire and its Commonwealth lasts for a thousand years, men will still say 'This was their finest hour'?"

Back in the darkest hours of Britain's wartime isolation Churchill clearly believed he knew his audience and what its courageous and generous response would be.

Much of such response germinated in Britain's traditional schools of the day where exhortations to sporting prowess and patriotism seldom fell on deaf ears.

Yet it might be salutary to ask ourselves here exactly how well Churchill's stirring words would be received and acted upon today?

Annals, August 2012

12

A NECESSARY DISTINCTION

The only people who don't think there is a problem with Islam are those who live on some other planet.

When a widely respected, humane and moderate journalist uses immoderate-seeming language such as the above surely it is high time for the rest of us to listen with due attention.

In the course of an article of close to 6,000 words in *The Weekend Australian* April 2-3, foreign news editor Greg Sheridan traced his transition from being an enthusiastic promoter of so-called multiculturalism to becoming a critic of what he sees now largely as national and international naivety and blindness in that regard.

Inevitably Sheridan has been labelled already as a racist for attempting to inject some overdue notions of sanity into future discussions of a sensitive subject. Being an intelligent and articulate man Sheridan would have been well aware in advance, of course, of the likelihood of such an ignorant and unhelpful response.

In Australia we claim to believe in free speech yet have subtle and unsubtle means at times of ensuring such freedom cannot occur. Yet Sheridan was at considerable pains to point out that his article was far from a blanket attack on any race or religion. Rather it was a considered criticism of misguided public policy and of a general failure by governments worldwide to grasp and deal with a problem that isn't likely to go away.

In Europe where Sheridan spent a recent month studying problems associated with widespread Muslim immigration an almost ubiquitous disenchantment with so-called multiculturalism now exists. As Sheridan explains: "German Chancellor Angela Merkel said recently Germany's attempt to create a multicultural society had failed completely. Britain's Prime Minister David Cameron recently denounced European-style multiculturalism saying: 'We have encouraged different cultures to live separate lives, apart from each other and apart from the mainstream. We've failed to provide a vision of society to which they feel they want to belong. We've even tolerated these segregated communities behaving in ways that run completely contrary to our values'. France's President Nicolas Sarkozy has agreed with Cameron and Merkel, that multiculturalism is a complete bust, as has Spain's former leader, Jose Maria Aznar".

Etymologically speaking multiculturalism belongs to a lexicon of so-called post-modernist virtues which have attempted to supersede and replace the values formerly associated with traditional Western societies. While most of such societies were once at least nominally Christian, today post-modernist initiatives of all kinds generally push the causes of secularism via thinly disguised waves of propaganda followed swiftly – as often as not – by some form of 'human rights' legislation.

The latter tactic is a none too subtle blending, in fact, of polemic, rhetoric and coercion.

An impression is given in short that all right-thinking people 'must' by now agree with the social and moral imperatives of, say, multiculturalism, feminism, relativism, political correctness, post-colonialism, gay marriage or a host of other 'isms' of relatively recent origin.

But as politicians and others often learn to their cost, while people may appear to agree with certain notions in public they often disagree with them very firmly in private.

Legislation such as anti-discriminatory laws thus often create an outward appearance of agreement while, in the meantime, the hearts and minds of a great many people may stay entirely unconvinced.

Australia which – in non-intellectual terms at least – is generally a quite generous country thus remains deeply ambivalent about the sort, condition and number of people we wish to welcome to these shores.

Imagined acceptance of multiculturalism thus provides a very inaccurate barometer of genuine public sentiment.

While widely spruiked as an undeniable virtue multiculturalism also has an undesirable undertow – to my mind at least – of less agreeable sentiments.

To paraphrase an old adage what multiculturalism appears to me to promote is the notion that any religion is as good as any other and that no religion is thus possibly the best option of all.

Hands up if you believe that is a desirable outcome.

Multiculturalism provides a very public slight, say, to Catholicism which has a long and honourable history of ethnic diversity in Australia. In some cases, at least, Catholic immigrants to Australia have fled persecutions by Muslims in their homelands. Why then should we welcome such present or potential persecutors of Christians here? One must presume the most likely answer to this is that Australia no longer regards itself as a Christian country.

Sheridan deals specifically with one of the salient factors that distinguish at least some Islamic institutions here very clearly from those of other faiths: "Many Australian Islamic institutions receive funding from Saudi Arabia, but I know from my work in Southeast Asia that the Saudis almost always fund an extremist interpretation of Islam.

To have concerns about these matters is not racism or xenophobia. It is reasonable.

It may be also that when young men of Islamic background experience failure and alienation they are much more readily prone to entrepreneurs of identity who offer them purpose through jihadi ideology, which has a large overlap with what they hear at the mosque and that they see on Arabic TV.

This is simply not true for Buddhists or Confucians or Sikhs or Jews or Christians, and to pretend so, to make all religions seem equal, is to deny reality.

Islam is a deep sea with a tradition of much spiritual goodness and genuine insight.

However, the Koran itself contains numerous injunctions to violent jihad and suppression of infidels".

Having been intrigued by Sheridan's extraordinarily long article I was naturally no less interested to discover how some readers at least of *The Australian* would react to his thesis via that paper's correspondence columns the following day.

The first letter to be printed was from a Dutchman who recounted in convincing detail

why he personally lost faith in multiculturalism owing to experiences in his homeland all of 25 years ago.

Predictably perhaps the next letter to be printed was from someone widely described – if certainly not by me – as 'Australia's leading public intellectual'. Preposterously Robert Manne compared Sheridan to the Nazi apologist Julius Streicher thus summing up, unintentionally, much of what is wrong and seemingly utterly and probably permanently hopeless about Australian intellectual life. Far from attempting to answer Sheridan's arguments constructively Manne – who occupies a very senior academic post in Victoria – reverted at once to the worst form of populist name-calling.

Actions such as the latter bring none of us closer to the answers we seek.

What many advocate in relation to immigration is that all who might wish to become legal immigrants not just to Australia but to a raft of other desirable 'host' nations should be compelled to undertake study not only of the national language but of how the host nation's principal national institutions operate as well as being asked to see the desirability of conforming to some form of over-arching national ethos as a necessary prelude to acceptance and citizenship. If would-be immigrants cannot or will not meet such minimal requirements many believe they should take their business elsewhere.

However, to state that does little more than scratch the surface of the problem. Almost all 'economic' migrants as well as genuine refugees would probably agree to more or less anything to gain acceptance. That said, the ability to remain in the host nation should sensibly be made dependant on certain forms of civic behaviour and this should be made clear to applicants from the outset. That is precisely where a sizable minority of Muslims in a variety of 'host' nations would almost certainly fail the test.

What such would-be immigrants need to enter into is a contract, in fact, in which in exchange for the gift of acceptance they are required to pledge a high degree of loyalty to national and democratic principles in return.

The matter of an over-arching form of national ethos is evidently much more complex and I am sympathetic here to would-be immigrants who, having survived undoubted hardships themselves, possibly see their Australian 'host' nation itself as becoming increasingly intellectually soft, materialistic and decadent itself.

Ironically the major cause of such intellectual and moral decadence is the set of post-modernist ideologies of which multiculturalism itself forms a far from negligible part.

Post-modernist ideologies are largely Marxist and thus atheistic in origin. Dedicated post-modernist ideologists therefore treat religions of all kinds largely as outmoded forms of superstition which at times interfere with or delay what they fondly imagine to be progress.

Unlike widely-shared religious notions of virtue which have generally stood the tests of time most adequately, post-modernist 'virtues' may, in time, come to be seen not as virtues at all but simply as semi-totalitarian attempts at social control.

If, as seems likely, the myth of multiculturalist virtue is due for imminent implosion one cannot help wondering which other recently invented post-modernist virtue may be next?

Annals, April/May 2011

13

THE WORLD TURNED UPSIDE DOWN

Courage is not simply one of the virtues but the form of every virtue at the testing point. C.S. Lewis

In an era in which every traditional virtue is likely to find itself challenged by some person or group from within the cosy physical and professional confines of one of Australia's universities, an odd coincidence brought just such an issue into especially sharp focus for me.

On the day on which the April issue of the Australian monthly magazine *Quadrant* arrived in my letterbox, I rediscovered a book I had mislaid since first reading it many months earlier on a return flight from England.

The book in question is a paperback which rightly achieved best-seller status. *First Light* by Geoffrey Wellum (Penguin Books 2003) is a first-hand account written by a former fighter pilot who began flying Spitfires during the Battle of Britain at the tender age of eighteen.

The author was in his late seventies when his book was published yet the freshness, modesty and humour of his account provides an intensely moving and credible story of the lives of otherwise ordinary young men who risked those lives on a daily basis.

Possibly Wellum's narrative was especially poignant for me because he was a pupil at a school which was a close local rival of the one I attended myself. Both of us were designated captains of cricket of our schools who were unable, for various reasons, to take up our appointments.

Wellum was half a generation older than I but I was at least an onlooker, as a small boy, of a good selection of the aerial warfare of the Second World War from the vantage point of my family's garden in Kent. Indeed, I recall to this day glorious summer skies full of hurtling, combatant aircraft.

While beautifully written and highly descriptive, Wellum's book is essentially a tale about the specifically military virtue of courage – although courage can admittedly take many other forms – and about the perennial debt which society should acknowledge towards those who displayed such virtue to an extraordinary extent on its behalf.

What then is the coincidental connection with the April edition of *Quadrant?*

The main feature article of that edition by Mervyn Bendle, who teaches at James Cook University, tells the story of a growing assault by certain Australian academics against all kinds of military tradition and against Anzac in particular. The article is appropriately called *A New Academic Onslaught against Anzac* and its author's brave exposure of this will undoubtedly place him offside with many of his university colleagues. In the same issue is another piece by regular columnist Peter Ryan who, like Wellum, began active wartime service at the age of eighteen – although in his case serving on his own behind Japanese lines in Papua New Guinea.

Ryan refers to the great military and civic virtue of stoicism and tells how aided he was in his wartime ordeals by such supreme historic exemplars of stoic philosophy as the Roman Marcus Aurelius.

Ryan also refers in his article to one from the January/February edition of *Quadrant* written by Dr.Michael Evans, who is a Fellow of the Australian Defence College in Canberra, which describes current Australian society as: "fundamentally unsympathetic to the profession of arms. The zeitgeist now wallows in the vacuities of post-modernism and in the insipid feebleness of moral relativity. What was once, with all its faults, a firm and familiar Australian culture is now a jellyfish, drifting aimless on seas of trendy hedonism. It has been reduced to this limp state very largely by the assaults, ignorance and neglect of its own schoolteachers and 'humanities' academics…"

Mervyn Bendle's article in *Quadrant* was triggered specifically by the recent publication of *What's Wrong with Anzac? The Militarisation of Australian History* (New South 2010) which is co-edited by Henry Reynolds and Marilyn Lake. Reynolds's name will be familiar to many from his involvement in the so-called 'history wars'. As Bendle explains "The book continually contrasts Anzac to the anti-war movement, with which the authors were directly involved or strongly identify…Consequently, the authors insist it is now high time 'to do justice to' Australia's anti-war tradition, by according it (and therefore themselves and their comrades) the same level of recognition as the Anzac tradition. This is an objective the Left has been pursuing at an international level for some twenty years, seeking to transform deserters, draft dodgers, anti-war activists and conscientious objectors into latter-day heroes, to be revered as much as the soldiers who actually faced frontline dangers in war".

Some may think, as I do, that Australia as a whole is discredited by the increasing decadence and corruption of young minds which flows out today into wider society – like ripples on a pond – from too many of its schools and universities. The increasing Left-wing politicisation of education here does nobody credit and should be resisted strenuously by all who value and would encourage the development of independent young minds.

Public education is a particular culprit here because in many instances parents have too little choice about where to send their children to school. How would you like your own children to be encouraged to become deserters at a time of national conflict especially if like me you have experienced military service yourself?

During my lifetime, courage – like honour and integrity – has increasingly departed the public scene with predictable consequences for society. In their place have come manufactured and purely supposed virtues such as political correctness which could at best be described as ersatz substitutes for the real thing.

What post-modernism has attempted to destroy above all is

moral certainty because in a rudderless and splintered society one philosophical idea may appear as good as any other – to the young and ignorant, at least – and no moral philosophy whatsoever possibly the best option of all.

Where universities were once looked on as repositories of academic and moral wisdom many seem today to have become instead promoters of the kind of total moral vacuum that Australia very sadly may eventually become.

Annals, June 2010

14

FLOODS, FIRES AND THE FLIGHT FROM REASON

During the past thirty years I have divided my time more or less equally between two contrasting locations.

From 1980 to 1995 I lived in England close beside the river Thames – which was formerly prone to flooding – whereas in Australia I managed somehow to choose a fire-prone area instead: the Upper Blue Mountains of New South Wales.

Both areas are truly beautiful and both have the advantage of easy access to the largest cities of their respective nations: in other words to London and Sydney.

At one time East Molesey, the precise location of my present and former abodes in England, was extremely liable to flood. As proof of this many of the older houses and shops still carry plaques which remind onlookers of the considerable heights reached by floods at various earlier moments in their histories.

The last major local flood occurred in 1968 however, and I remember the occasion well because my parents had moved to the area some years earlier. After weeks of heavy rain, a vast deluge of water disgorged itself into the Thames uncomfortably close to their house. This torrent of muddy water had travelled cross-country from another river, inundating a busy shopping street on its way.

The basic problem was that the entire area was low-lying and was served by not just one river but three – the Thames, the Mole and the Ember – all of which converge rather inconveniently at a point noted for venerable buildings such as Hampton Court Palace.

In 1963 the Thames had frozen over at that precise point, for the first time in over a century, whereas in 1987 the river carried white-tipped breakers instead which were whipped up by the infamous hurricane of that year which went on to flatten some 15 million trees – the worst such great gale in England since the distant days of 1703.

I was present in person on each of these three occasions of 'extreme' weather and cannot help wondering whether, if that trio of events had happened today, they might not all be attributed to that universal, meteorological scapegoat of our times known as 'global warming'.

Back in 1963, 1968 and 1987, however, nobody dreamt of offering such a lame excuse for the inconveniences which nature sometimes provides.

What was realised instead, after the floods of 1968, was that a major flood prevention scheme was needed to protect the householders of a flood-prone residential area. In the ensuing years the sound of pile-drivers became if not music to local residents' ears then at least indications of relief to come as the unruly waters of the Mole and Ember were slowly contained and disciplined by strategically placed weirs.

At the seaward end of the Thames, in the meantime, a truly massive project had been undertaken, known today as the Thames Barrier. Its basic aim was to protect the residents of Britain's capital from incoming surges by the sea – an aim which it has subsequently delivered with total success.

Both projects were completed and officially opened for service in 1982. What was thus recognised in England, at least, was that householders deserve some degree of protection against the elements via the authorities of the state.

I take the slight liberty here of contrasting such a state of affairs with the one which continues to prevail in the Blue Mountains where my wife and I still retain a home.

At the moment of writing both of us have had little sleep as we monitor events each night regarding daytime happenings in the Blue

Mountains where exceptional bushfires have been raging, more or less out of control, for a week or more.

Nobody disputes the vast powers of natural forces, especially in Australia, but neither should we underestimate the powers of human ingenuity when these are harnessed to genuine determination and purpose.

The first thing that needs saying here is that the magnitude of the fires in the Blue Mountains has nothing whatsoever to do with 'global warming' – even if such a phenomenon could legitimately be said to exist.

What they reflect, in fact, is that for too many years the local bush has not been properly maintained: fire-breaks and fire-trails have become overgrown, insufficient back-burning and clearing have taken place and – amazingly on the face of it – residents are often actively discouraged by those in authority from properly maintaining their blocks.

In a fire-prone country such as Australia it is also sheer madness, of course, to allow fuel loads to escalate to dangerous levels.

Has part of the human race therefore suddenly conceived a death wish? Or does some other, equally bizarre explanation exist which may account for such suicidal-seeming behaviour?

When communism collapsed in Eastern Europe nearly a quarter of a century ago now that event might have seemed to leave many radical Western intellectuals not just with egg on their faces but without any obvious new radical cause to espouse.

What possible polemical cause could they embrace which would enable them to tell the rest of us once again that we were 'doing it all wrong'?

In short, how on earth were they going to appear much more publicly righteous once again than the rest of us?

Some years ago I wrote a piece called 'Ecological Marxism and Other Delights' for the pages of this journal.

In it I cited an article by the Hon. Kevin Andrews called *Revolutionary Ambitions of the Greens*. Andrews quotes former leader of the Builders

Labourers Federation Jack Munday, who was instrumental in the development of Green politics in Australia, as seeing Green politics as "ecological Marxism". That was not just because considerations of the environment or ecology must be placed before all else according to him but because such ideological-sounding causes should be pursued *where necessary by totalitarian means.*

Andrews goes on "The Greens belief in their ecological nirvana manifests itself in a new coercive utopianism: unless we understand the ideological foundations of the Greens, we will fail to effectively address the challenge of their revolution".

What Andrews is at least hinting at here is that Greens who are often 'rebadged' Marxists are no great respecters of the processes of democracy. Their influence is correspondingly much greater than their levels of public support might suggest – especially perhaps on local councils.

A major backlash is overdue now against the excesses of Green policies of the immediate past. Contrary to their beliefs they are not the sole people who love their environment. Many others of us do but we would also prefer to conduct our lives in some sensible degree of safety. On at least five occasions since living in the mountains our property has come under imminent and – in the long run – quite unnecessary threats from fire.

Local, state and federal governments are not fulfilling their duties to their citizens by allowing this to continue to happen.

A friend who lives near me in the mountains owns a pre-war street guide which indicates that a local road known now as Cliff Drive was known formerly as Scenic View Drive. At one time, in other words, the road was properly maintained since magnificent views from it were formerly uninterrupted. Today this same road, which runs along the top of the escarpment, has no views at all because scruffy gum trees grow right to one edge of the road where they interface with the tall trees growing on its other side – thus providing an ideal conduit for possible fire in a built-up residential area.

Such slackness is to be found almost anywhere today in the Blue

Mountains and indicates local government which has – in the face of Green pressures – largely lost the plot.

Local schoolchildren have been told the Blue Mountains 'megafire' was entirely due to 'global warming'.

The rest of us have very good reason to hold rather a different view.

Annals, October 2013

15

PLEASE DON'T TELL THE THOUGHT POLICE

On nights when I can't sleep I often find myself reflecting with pleasure on my latter days of playing serious cricket – on a number of occasions with players who went on to become international stars.

Just one of these was the West Indian opening batsman Gordon Greenidge who combined prodigious talent with a truly charming and sunny personality even at a young age.

In days before political correctness blighted the lives of sportsmen – along with those of almost everyone else – Gordon was nevertheless sometimes the butt of typical cricketers' jokes some of which would undoubtedly be deemed racist today and probably reported to some form or other of self-righteous civic authority.

Thus if the light became dim while our side was fielding someone or other was almost bound to remark "Give us a smile Gordon so we can see where you are" – a time-honoured quip with which a great many black cricketers were once very likely to be familiar.

I do not think Gordon or any other sensible young man of our day would have been in the least offended by this. Many of us had known military service in those days where humour was most likely to be somewhat ruder and blacker than this.

Indeed Gordon was entirely capable of turning jokes neatly himself even when these involved topics possibly now regarded as taboo.

On one occasion he and I attempted to break an existing record for two men pulling a 'light' iron roller around the entire perimeter of a sloping cricket ground – Lulworth Castle in Dorset – against the clock.

After our narrowly unsuccessful but utterly gut-wrenching attempt Gordon retreated behind the cricket pavilion where he vomited for some minutes before eventually emerging absolutely ashen-faced to rejoin the rest of us.

"I think that's the nearest I will ever come to being a white man" he remarked to our relieved applause.

Today, forty years on, we live in a world in which a variety of social ideologies such as political correctness masquerade as virtues when they are nothing of the kind. Political correctness is, in fact, the first cousin of political 'spin' but is even more insidious since it is designed to fly under the radar of normal public consciousness.

Unfortunately, in what has become an increasingly unconfident and confused society, many lack the ability now to spot the difference between self-righteousness and virtue – an unfortunate problem which seems to have haunted the human race at least since the days of the New Testament.

At best, political correctness is an attempted form of social control which may alter apparent behaviour while leaving basic attitudes untouched. Frequently its advocates go to absurd extremes which defeat their own ends. In London a few years ago I passed a pub which advertised the availability there of 'a ploughperson's lunch'. I could only hope its management was simply being ironic.

I count myself very fortunate indeed to have reached adulthood before the advent of political correctness or of any of the many 'isms' which together constitute that amorphous entity called post-modernism which today seeks to control – whether we like it or not – much of the general conduct of our lives.

Great numbers of people exist now, in short, who have never experienced any genuine form of social normality.

What has been destroyed most damagingly for great numbers of people is individual and communal moral certainty. Typically they are told something is right and fair but do not in their bones believe it to be so. They are victims in other words of a cultural and moral revolution in which they – like most of the rest of us – never had much say.

Unlike many great religions of the world, post-modernism is a worldwide phenomenon of very recent origin and does not, in any case, tap into any of the moral traditions which underwrote the great civilisations of the past. Indeed, a major world religion such as Christianity is quite likely to find itself – along with the sublime artistic and architectural achievements it once fostered – dismissed today by our new moral masters as either anachronistic or superstitious. The world they desire is an atheistic one in which the social commandments they are so keen to issue replace those once handed down to us by God.

Post-modernism in its various forms and guises is a product of the so-called counter-culture of the Sixties which attempted to subvert all forms of traditional morality not through political revolution – which would never have succeeded – but through the effective ideological capture of such cornerstones of our civilisation as education and culture. Today – outside private and Church schools – secondary education, as it would have been understood by people of my generation, can scarcely be said to exist.

The American cultural commentator Roger Kimball summarised this whole situation with great accuracy in the following way: "That ideology has insinuated itself, disastrously, into the curricula of our schools and colleges; it has significantly altered the texture of sexual relations and family life; it has played havoc with the authority of churches and other repositories of moral wisdom; it has undermined the claims of civic virtue and our national self-understanding; it has degraded the media, the entertainment industry, and popular culture; it has helped to subvert museums and other institutions entrusted with preserving and transmitting high culture. It has even, most poignantly, addled our hearts and innermost assumptions about what counts as the good life: it has perverted our dreams as much as it has prevented us from attaining them".

Elsewhere in the same excellent book from which the above quotation was taken – *The Long March* (Encounter Books 2000) – Kimball makes the following equally astute observations: "For over two hundred years, the Left has had an effective but unearned monopoly on the rhetoric of virtue…As with most revolutions, the counterculture's call for total freedom quickly turned into a demand for total control. The phenomenon of 'political correctness', with its speech codes and other efforts to enforce ideological conformity, was one predictable result of this transformation. What began at the University of California at Berkeley with the Free Speech Movement soon degenerated into an effort to abridge freedom by dictating what could and could not be said about any number of politically sensitive issues".

Political correctness had its origins less than 50 years ago on the other side of the world yet has infiltrated the behavioural norms of almost every Western nation including Australia and is frequently backed now by punitive forms of civil legislation.

Racism which is contrary, of course, to civilised Christian behaviour is now accorded the status of serious crime while all sorts of other offences against traditional morality often find themselves airbrushed away – highly conveniently – via a series of politically correct euphemisms.

The late Frank Devine, who was one of my valued former colleagues at *The Australian*, wrote once that he found class hatred every bit as objectionable as racial hatred but I sense that not too many contemporary Australians will have fully appreciated the wisdom of his words.

So why is class hatred more apparently acceptable here than race hatred?

The reason is that the whole basis for the post-modernist counterculture which now effectively rules our lives is founded in neo-Marxist ideology – of which 'class' warfare, along with anti-religious sentiment is, of course, a cornerstone.

Race hatred thus becomes elevated way above class hatred as a civic crime in societies, such as that of Australia, in which post-modernist ideologies such as political correctness now increasingly rule us.

But that is not the sole reason.

Multiculturalism, of course, is another of the principal planks of the whole insidious post-modernist platform. According to multiculturalist ideology no race or religion is more desirable or superior to any other. Therefore all kinds of immigrant, for example, should be welcomed equally to our shores.

In an ideal world, at least, the sheer humanitarianism of this argument seems beyond reproach. But regrettably this particular argument may well conceal a hidden agenda.

Prior to post-modernism the dominant social ideology of Western countries was almost always some form of secularised Christianity and it is precisely that which post-modernism seeks to overthrow and eventually to eliminate altogether. Therefore the more such ideology can be diluted through an influx of non-Christian or even anti-Christian immigrants the better.

Skin colour has thus become merely a convenient smokescreen.

In short it is not people's race that matters but what, if anything, they essentially and strongly believe. Christians like Hindus, Muslims, Buddhists or Orthodox Jews generally – and understandably – feel most comfortable when living among their own kind. The entire history of the world so far supports this view.

Of course, mutually tolerant communities can co-exist and should be encouraged to do so but that is not necessarily an entirely 'natural' answer.

The strongest proponents of multiculturalism are often atheists who dismiss all forms of religious belief as anachronistic or even absurd

Thus such people would at least pretend not to understand why a devout Catholic, say, might prefer to live in the Republic of Ireland rather than in Pakistan.

Like so many aspects of postmodernism the whole thing really is just about as silly as that.

Annals, March 2010

16

CAUSE AND EFFECT IS HARDLY ROCKET SCIENCE

Someone remarked to me once that it is the mark of a second-rate mind that it cannot properly grasp the implications of its own arguments.

As the years pass by the wisdom of that remark becomes more and more apparent to me.

For example, 40 years or so after the advent of a variety of supposedly world-changing postmodernist initiatives we see that a number of these have created precisely the adverse social effects a person of sense and experience might have expected from the outset.

But that, in a sense, is the least of our worries. What is really frightening is that what began as examples of immature ideology have seemingly become transformed somehow over the passage of time and now enjoy the status of received wisdom.

Indeed who argues today in Australia against the notion that feminism, political correctness, multiculturalism and environmentalism, say, or relaxation of the laws of censorship have been anything but beneficial in creating a kind of society here which imagines it leads the world in 'progress' and enlightenment.

Yet even as we congratulate ourselves on the advanced nature of our thinking and societal state we are regularly brought up short by unpleasant and apparently unforeseen social eruptions such as endemic bullying in our schools. How can this possibly happen in a 'perfect' society such as ours?

As those bringing us news of such eruptions scratch their

heads, 'expert' academic commentators are wheeled in on our TV programmes to explain such contrary phenomena to the rest of us.

Why do such worrying problems continue to occur even in wonderful, present-day Australia?

Refreshingly one such expert made an overdue admission recently that "people in Australia behave less well towards each other than they used to."

Unfortunately that particular commentator was not asked why she believed the latter to be the case but I hope her answer might have included some reference to a decline in the presence or influence of traditional moral teaching – a decline which begins in our schools and universities and then spreads out into society generally.

I do not suggest for a moment here that children of my own generation always behaved well but rather *that most of them understood quite clearly when they were behaving badly* whether to their fellow pupils or to society in general. Teachers, parents and older schoolmates were often quick to assist them in this understanding.

By contrast, I believe that vast numbers of children in Australian schools have very little grasp even of elementary morality today at least partly because they have become confused and anxiety-ridden by being invited by their teachers to share in feelings of collective guilt towards Australia's earliest inhabitants or because of mankind's supposed part in the imminent destruction of our planet.

Even at the most elementary psychological level it is clear that burdening children with utterly unjustified guilt is never salutary and a loss of confidence in the moral judgements of teachers could thus be merely one obvious side effect of this.

So how do we even begin to explain endemic bullying in Australian schools or, to move on to a more grown-up context, equally deplorable levels of adult violence and sexual assaults?

Traditionally those who oppose any kind of censorship or self-imposed restraint argue that violent, amoral and semi-pornographic material does negligible harm to anyone. In fact, to interfere with its transmission, publication or proliferation is, in their view, an unacceptable curtailment of human freedom.

Off-hand, other than equally mendacious claims made for the human and social benefits of communism, I can think of no other area of human untruth which is so widely promoted as the notion that violent and pornographic material can ever be harmless.

At best it could be argued that both kinds of material 'merely' brutalise and deprave – whereas at worst it has been demonstrated time and again that serial rapists, say, are likely to be avid consumers of pornographic material. In short, any material which brutalises and depraves can never be harmless.

While some parents, at least, are vigilant in the case of their own children's possible exposure to gratuitously violent or pornographic material at home myriad outside opportunities exist today for exposure via computers and computer games.

For children who come already from dysfunctional and violent homes, exposure to brutal or salacious material simply endorses attitudes to life and society which may already be burgeoning in a sad absence of contrary influences. For children of low or limited intelligence differences between fact and fantasy are also notoriously hard to establish.

The real reason why we are 'treated' to so much gratuitously violent and salacious material on our television screens is, of course, because a 'ratings' war exists between rival stations in their unending quest for the advertisers' dollar. Public taste has therefore been 'educated' to accept worse and worse material and it would be foolish to assume that any end is in sight yet from this downward spiral. What Australian television programs may be like in 10 years time bears little thinking about.

Yet oddly our post-modernist world is wildly inconsistent over questions of control. While too little is done in my view to curtail the availability and endless proliferation of violent and pornographic material on the grounds that to do so might infringe 'important' human liberties, such desirable – and harmless- human freedoms as the right to decide what sort of trees and shrubs one wishes to grow in one's own garden are under frequent attack now from environmentalist busybodies.

Just how mad can we get?

You may not wish to answer that question.

A friend who lives in a North Sydney suburb told me recently that the passing of planning applications there carries stipulations about what will or will not be permitted to be grown in the adjacent garden.

Indeed, in the area where I live myself an attempt was made a few years ago to introduce a *Vegetation Management Order or VMO* whereby householders would be obliged to seek the permission of the local council even to relocate any plant of a metre or more in height within the confines of their own property. Neighbours were even encouraged to 'grass' – if you will forgive the pun – on any seen to be breaking this absurd piece of vegetal totalitarianism.

What sort of society is it which makes little or no attempt to control harmful 'freedoms' while conducting simultaneous assaults on completely harmless ones?

The answer to that is not an altogether encouraging one I'm afraid.

Annals, April/May 2011

17

THE EU: THE NEXT UTOPIAN DREAM TO COLLAPSE?

To Australians in general – and those of European extraction especially – much that takes place in Europe these days must seem incomprehensible or even bizarre.

The physical distance that separates Australia from Europe could be thought to be a factor here yet – even for those of us who live in much greater proximity to it – the workings of the vast bureaucratic enterprise known as the European Union still often seem to make little or no sense.

At the time of writing for example, the British press is full of comment about an admission just made by Britain's former Labour Home Secretary Jack Straw that his government's decision in 2004 to let Eastern European migrants come to Britain to work was 'a spectacular mistake' – one other, brighter European nations somehow managed to avoid. The expected influx was apparently 5,000 to 13,000 a year – a somewhat lower estimate, you may agree, than the average annual arrival of some 100,000, peaking at double that – which has actually transpired over the past ten years.

One cannot help wondering sometimes about the expertise of at least some British government advisors.

Before setting out any further examples of apparent folly, however, I feel it might be more constructive to recall words said to me as a very young man by someone considerably older and wiser: "It is the mark of second-rate minds that they cannot foresee the implications of their proposals".

Here is a notion that is certainly worth thinking about in relation to the EU.

During my subsequent life I have witnessed a great many instances of this particular maxim in action. Usually such examples involve utopian social engineering of some kind and almost always involve a total disregard of the realities of human nature – thus sowing the twin seeds necessary for future collapse.

The European Union takes a lofty and often high-handed tone towards the roughly 400 million folk who fall into its ambit. Yet frequently its social, economic and agricultural policies seem muddled and misguided although that, to my mind, is possibly the least of our worries.

The much greater concern is that the unelected bureaucrats of the European Union have by now come to see themselves as the effective inventors and guardians of a new morality which transcends all former national frontiers and beliefs. In general this supposed moral code is a mish-mash of those post-modernist ideas with which we have become all too familiar: equal opportunities, anti-discrimination, gay rights, political correctness, multiculturalism, feminism, abortion virtually on demand and so forth. Wherever these clash with Christian – and especially with traditional Catholic beliefs – these new imperatives now take precedence, generally under a generic but misleading rubric of 'human rights'.

Oddly all such novel dictates are then presented to us as though they were quasi-religious absolutes in themselves even though all, of course, are atheistic and sometimes profoundly irreligious in nature.

After two millennia of being ordered by what can best be described perhaps as 'secularised Christianity' modern Europe now faces being forced to accept a novel, entirely man-made moral code much of which derives, in the last analysis, from the ponderings of Marx.

In an article in Britain's *The Daily Telegraph* (19.11.2013) Lord Carey, former Anglican Archbishop of Canterbury states his belief that "Christianity" – by which I assume he simply means the Anglican Church – "is at risk now of dying out within a generation". If he is right then novel 'Euro-morality' must surely take a fair share of the blame.

For Britain most of the attraction of belated acceptance into the European Union lay in the access this provided to European markets which apparently absorb up to 50% of our exports. I do not question the idealism of a least some of the original European concept yet hugely regret its effect, in Britain's case, on our relationship with Commonwealth countries which are probably our more natural and historic allies.

In another recent article culled from Britain's *The Daily Telegraph* (14.11.2013) Peter Oborne, a reliable British commentator, makes an excellent job of explaining what has gone wrong with the European Union since its rosy beginnings: "Almost all of us value free trade, international cooperation and mutual goodwill. None of us wants to return to the bloodshed of earlier centuries. In recent years, however, Europe has fallen under the control of a new ruling class that has obtained powers which it has no democratic right to exercise. Think of it like this: the European Union has abolished politics. Highly susceptible to lobby groups and large corporations, it is now out of reach to political parties and national politicians. This is far more dangerous than has yet been realised. Again and again national leaders are finding themselves accountable for decisions they haven't made and can't alter. Let's take the example of the single currency, which seemed such a good idea to EU bosses. The abolition of national currencies means that states can no longer manage their own economies, and are governed instead by international bankers, in cooperation with Brussels commissioners. This is the cause of social and political collapse in Greece, Spain, Italy and Portugal".

Oborne is absolutely right here. But there were other fatal flaws in the whole European enterprise which managed to get overlooked almost from the outset.

In short, the history of individual European nation states is not distinguished solely by their propensity to fight each other but through their historic development of distinctive constitutions, legislatures and cultures. A large-scale trading alliance is therefore one thing – such alliances have existed successfully in history – while a binding legislative alliance which rides roughshod over ingrained national characteristics, histories, cultures and even types of national ability is clearly something else which no amount of ideological murmuring can dispel in the long run.

Thus two of the major progenitors of the European Union, Konrad Adenauer and Charles de Gaulle, were united not just via their devout personal Catholicism and belief in the family unit rather than the state as the essential building- block of society but by a mutual dislike and distrust – even though they were recent military foes themselves – of Britain.

Both also faced very significant presences of communist parties in their national elections, something Britain managed to avoid, ostensibly at least, since in Britain communism played a more covert role. That lay in the destruction of national industry and thus, by inference, of national economic growth. Germany has therefore consistently outperformed Britain and all other European nations economically with the occasional exception of France.

Among older generations of Britons, at least, dislike of EU membership has generally become profound by now.

In a recent case, a failed asylum-seeker from Sudan who entered Britain illegally was subsequently sentenced to prison here for sexual activity with a child and was due to be deported. An immigration tribunal then decided it would breach the European Convention on Human Rights to do so as he might face persecution if returned to the Sudan. So far the case has cost the UK taxpayer the equivalent of half a million Australian dollars and the convicted paedophile is now likely to receive compensation worth tens of thousands of dollars because of the efforts of Britain's Home Office to deport him. The parents of his 13 year old female victim are understandably 'unimpressed'.

As I seek to conclude this article a case involving thousands rather than a solitary individual has further aroused national fury here. From 1 January 2014 Britain has been ordered by the European Court of

Justice to open its borders and employment markets to migrants from Romania and Bulgaria. Up to 70,000 are expected each year at a time of high unemployment here among young people and health and education systems which are stretched already beyond breaking point. So-called 'Roma' immigrants from Slovakia, who are entirely unaccustomed to urban life, have already been the cause of near riots in an important British city.

In the meantime, even highly-qualified English-speaking Australians are finding it extremely difficult either to work or gain permanent residence here, even when married to British nationals.

Perhaps I should leave the last words here to a fellow Australian, as reported by British columnist Allison Pearson: "The other night I was seated at dinner next to Mike Rann, the Australian High Commissioner to the UK. I asked him to tell me what he thought about turning away Australians. Without missing a beat he said: "Whenever Britain has been in trouble, without even needing to be asked, Australia has been the first by your side. We fought and died with you because we regard you as family."

If modern Europe is indeed supposed to be a 'family' it is by now an extremely unhappy and divided one.

Annals, November 2013

18

THE NEXT CATHOLIC IN KIRRIBILLI?

In his recently published and strongly selling book *Battlelines* (Melbourne University Press 2009 $34.99) Catholic politician Tony Abbott expounds his personal vision of what he believes the conservative side of politics should continue to foster and embrace.

In the course of 182 pages he explains why he holds the opinions he does largely through autobiographical anecdotes, a brief summary of recent Australian political events and a welcome peek at what conservatism – or liberal/conservatism – has meant to other political thinkers in different lands and times.

The author also attempts to foresee ways in which a conservative philosophy can contribute to a brighter and more stable future for his fellow Australians.

Since I am about to become one of the latter myself, I am also one of a growing population of people Mr.Abbott needs to convince by his arguments.

The fact that he has taken time out from a very busy and demanding life to deliver his reasoning at some length argues for the author's evident sincerity and self-belief. Indeed, here the author's decency and lack of bombast may help explain why a complementary sense of personal destiny seems strangely absent from his text. Mr.Abbott writes well and argues clearly but he does not really write like a man who has felt God's hand rest – even fleetingly – on his political shoulder.

At heart I sense a slight but fundamental confusion in the author's aims.

Abbott's autobiographical notes hint sometimes at a man who can be unworldly or even naïve – in spite of an outwardly tough and often charismatic exterior – and this does not augur well in imagined future tanglings with leaders of some of the world's worst totalitarian regimes.

Perhaps the most interesting aspect of his autobiography dwells tellingly on his near embrace, at an earlier stage in his life, of religious vocation as a priest and thus as a servant of a more specific and readily identifiable community. Instead, Mr.Abbott turned, for unusually admirable reasons, to a career in political life.

What worries me in such a context is not whether Abbott is a good or worthy enough man but whether he is sharply focused enough to attain and maintain the highest peak in his alternative calling.

The author is at his best and most generous when writing of the sound organisation and thoughtful management techniques of the previous Howard/Costello government and when he contrasts such considerate and effective methods with what he sees as the frenetic, pseudo-symbolic and often near-tyrannical methods of our present federal rulers from the ALP.

Mr.Abbott paints John Howard as a political thinker from the mould of Edmund Burke, going so far as to invoke Burke's beautiful metaphor of society as "a partnership between the living, the dead and the yet unborn".

Conservatism, like the Catholic church, is founded on the vital human principle of continuity. Its true adherents should never forget this.

In just such a context, the author explains why Edmund Burke (1729-1797) supported the American Revolution – because it was an attempt to regain in the new world the traditional rights and freedoms of Englishmen – yet trenchantly opposed the French Revolution which he saw as a usurpation of established order in the name of abstract principles that was bound to lead to tyranny.

For Burke, the greatest evil of the French Revolution lay in its overturning of all precedent.

One can imagine that if Burke were alive today he would also abhor utterly – as I do – the example the French Revolution later provided Lenin and Stalin in deliberate and unbridled use of terror.

In short, the French, who include my paternal ancestors, have a great deal to answer for.

Abbott argues convincingly on the necessity to temper political ideology with everyday commonsense and related pragmatic instincts for political survival.

He also echoes, by odd coincidence, the precise criticism of socialism made by my late, Hungarian-born friend Andras Kalman which I quoted in the June edition of *Annals*: "before we start dividing wealth it first makes sense to create it".

Abbott's text repeats this same cogent sentiment at somewhat greater length: "It's much easier to redistribute wealth to the needy if wealth is being created. Wealth creation means that there can be more for everyone rather than an ugly fight to take away what some people already have. In countries with market economies, successful Labor leaders normally understand that 'soak the rich' policies can be taken only so far; although their supporters often don't."

In short, socialism which masquerades – or, more politely, likes to present itself – as the politics of 'fairness' is too often nothing more today, in fact, than the straightforward politics of envy.

So far as it impinges on most people's lives, conservatism often manifests itself through socio-economic consequences which include stability, small government, low taxation, personal freedom via absence of excessive bureaucratic interference and a healthy respect for law and order.

To me, at least, all of the above register as traditional as well as political virtues rather than vices.

Today the strongest opposition to conservative – or traditional – values comes not from a disenfranchised proletariat nor from blue-collar battlers but rather from a self-appointed intellectual class drawn largely from academia, teachers, public service employees, the media and the arts. Significantly, few of the foregoing produce physical end-products from their labours and are thus generally affected less and more loosely than most others by possible fluctuations in our economy.

Modern socialism also likes to present itself not just as an ideology of 'fairness' – whatever such a word, in a world of widely differing degrees of human motivation and ability could properly be held to mean – but also of 'progress', another word used almost entirely today in rhetorical contexts.

Indeed, at the recently held national conference of the ALP a female delegate argued that Australians would surely soon embrace same-sex marriages on the grounds of our traditional national love of 'fairness' rather than on the equally problematic rhetorical grounds of 'progress'.

Indeed, that such an argument may succeed in modern Australian life is possibly an even greater reflection on the role played by a poorly educated and largely uninterested section of the electorate than that of the politicians who nominally represent such people.

One of the major dangers facing conservative politics not just in Australia but in Western countries generally is precisely the kind of issue I have outlined above where a temptation to placate a significant minority may alienate an equally large body of traditional voters.

The vexed subject of supposed 'climate change' is another obvious case in point during the debates about which alarming quantities of toxic argument have been released already into our atmosphere.

I fear sensible debate may never really recover from that shock.

Annals, August 2009

19

STILL WORTH A LOOK?

At one time young Australians – of British and European extraction especially – tended to tour the lands associated with their ancestral roots more or less automatically as soon as they could find the funds to do so.

More recently, however, I sense there has been an at least slight falling off of this particular form of youthful enterprise not just through increased costs and difficulties of travel but because at least some have been persuaded by their elders that Australia is by now just about the most remarkable, blessed and wisely run country in human history. Is anywhere else therefore – other than Bali, Gallipoli and some favoured parts of the USA perhaps – really worth even a look?

Do I exaggerate here?

Not long before I returned to Europe last year, an Australian-born rural solicitor explained to me why he had left his native New South Wales only once during his relatively long life – and Australia never at all. That was because he knew already that he lived in the world's finest possible place – so what was the real point of visiting anywhere else since it was bound to be 'inferior'?

I have wondered subsequently whether his lack of geographical curiosity extended also to history. In short, because of the supposed wonders and enlightenment of our present technological age why should other ages be of interest to us?

Ironically, in view of the foregoing, I must confess that after 17 years of living in Australia it was the historic resonance and variety of British and European cities, towns and villages – and of their surrounding countryside – that I found I missed most.

Since my return to England last year I have perhaps over-compensated, rushing out almost every weekend to explore yet another of the ancient castles, manor houses and historic gardens that lie within relatively easy reach of where we presently live.

Indeed, within an hour and a half's comfortable drive lie at least fifty extraordinary architectural attractions most of which belong by now to a reformed and much improved organisation: Britain's National Trust.

Twenty years ago I can recall a frequent bossiness and sense of condescension among their guides as though some of these were showing you round their own houses rather than priceless buildings belonging to the nation. All of this seems to have improved greatly in my absence. Today, belonging to the National Trust is one of very few bargains on offer in British life and the guides they currently employ seem on the whole modest, informed and extremely helpful.

For an annual subscription for two equivalent to about AU $130 we have already visited over twenty historic properties enjoying free entry to car parks, gardens and the buildings themselves. Most are open except for the coldest winter months and while a preponderance of visitors may be middle-aged or older, it is also heartening to see many more children than I remember from previous times learning at least something about their nation's history.

At one time most would have been assured of encouragement in this at their schools but too often that is no longer the case. In general this is because of the increasing politicisation of secondary education in all except fee-paying or religious schools.

Recent surveys conducted in state schools in Britain often reveal staggering levels of historical ignorance.

I have written in these pages already of a recent visit I made to Chartwell, Sir Winston Churchill's former country retreat.

On a visit to the surrounding Kentish Weald a few weeks earlier, a lone Spitfire had appeared flying suddenly up a wooded valley at low altitude and I found myself transported back for an instant to the days of my childhood when wartime aerial combats were often visible from the back garden of our family home. From there I also saw one of the very first flying bombs or 'doodlebugs' en route to London towards the end of the Second World War. Its strange contours and the vibrations occasioned by its primitive jet engine – which caused the palings of our garden fence to rattle ominously – marked it out for me instantly as something I had never seen before.

Churchill, as I well realise, is often criticised roundly in Australia despite his definitive role in the Second World War yet remains, to my mind, a more historically reputable figure by far than the American President of the day F.D.Rooseveldt not least because of the nature of the latter's wartime dealings with Stalin and the woeful effect these had on the subsequent shape of post-war Europe.

Chartwell lies in idyllic pastoral surroundings close to the charming Kentish town of Westerham. The Kentish Weald was once a densely forested area and while that is no longer the case the lack of intrusive buildings visible from Chartwell remains astonishing for a location so close to the nation's capital. A cluster of equally important and much earlier historic buildings more or less surrounds Chartwell and the pretty nearby town of Sevenoaks.

Prominent among these is Knole built in 1454 by the then Archbishop of Canterbury and which remains one of the largest private houses in England. Knole was the traditional home of the Sackville family and still gives its name internationally to a form of drop-ended couch once used to accommodate visiting military personnel overnight. Not far down the road lies Hever Castle, a moated fortification dating back still earlier to the late 13th century. Hever was the girlhood home of the ill-fated Anne Boleyn (1507-36), second queen of Henry VIII. In the early 20th century Hever was acquired by William Waldorf Astor who created a vast Italian garden there with accompanying lake. To complete a quartet of utterly remarkable buildings, Penshurst Place boasts an extraordinary Great Hall dating from 1360 and was the traditional home of ancestors of Sir Philip Sidney (1554-86) whose successors were not without significance, of course, in the subsequent history of Australia. Incredibly all four buildings lie roughly within a

12 x 12 kilometre square.

When visiting such buildings it feels impossible for me not to sense history's hand resting heavily on my shoulder. In the grounds of such houses well recorded historical events become much easier to imagine; passages of history no longer seem remote or dubious, in fact, but almost palpable. For instance, when the walls of Hever Castle were being built, the Norman invasion of England lay little more than 200 years in the past. Indeed, when the Battle of Hastings took place in 1066 the world-changing events of the New Testament were themselves little more than a thousand years distant.

At the moment of writing there seems no shadow of doubt that the Battle of Hastings took place 946 years ago, although interestingly its precise location has very recently been called into question. And while that famous battle took place in East Sussex there seems equally little historical doubt that St.Augustine landed in the neighbouring county of Kent some 469 years before that in 597AD. He was under orders from Pope Gregory the Great to convert the heathen English to Christianity – a process which is surely no less necessary today. Where he landed in Kent was just about at the nearest point to France.

Many unbelievers act today as though the history of Christianity is somehow largely a matter of fable and myth while seeming, at the same time, to experience no difficulty at all in acknowledging much older histories of events in Egypt, say – or that of Australia's Aborigines.

More or less wherever one wanders in Britain there are obvious signs of the making of the country's history as well as strange relics which quicken our curiosity. Discovering details of one's family history can also open doors to historical realisation although, in my own case, to the unwelcome discovery that the history of my father's family reaches back to notable heretics in 13th century Southern France.

Should you come to England in the next few years, another brace of buildings I recommend thoroughly – to lovers of gardens especially – are the famous Elizabethan mansion at Sissinghurst which was lovingly restored in the 1930s and the less well known Great Dixter, owned until quite recently by an Australian, which boasts the wildest and most profuse formal gardens I have ever seen. In the meantime, its superb half-timbered manor house probably looks externally very much as it did in 1450. So, also does a very similar but slightly later house, Smallhythe Place, which was bought by the actress Ellen Terry in 1902. That house has been preserved exactly as she left it and the tiny theatre she built in a barn still remains in use to this day.

Do any of the foregoing tempt you?

If exploring the Kent/Sussex borders do not on any account miss the glorious, largely half-timbered village of Chilham – where I first learnt to paint – or the coastal town of Rye.

The novelist Henry James lived there at Lamb House, a residence and grounds so perfect for any writer that for me at least his prolific output is at long last amply explained.

** Britain's National Trust currently administers over 300 historic buildings and more than 200 famous gardens.*

Annals, November 2013

20

RATHER A DIFFERENT BRITAIN

Change and decay in all around I see;
O Thou, who changest not, abide with me.
(Henry Francis Lyte 1793-1847)

Are you familiar with the famous British magazine *Country Life?*

Such copies of that excellent country journal which I have managed to buy in Australia seem always to be a bit out of date yet the core of the dream that publication peddles remains essentially unchanging.

Informed articles on subjects such as haymaking, wild birds, country crafts and working dogs aside, much of the attraction the magazine provides lies in the glossy advertising it carries for idyllic rural properties. These may be located almost anywhere in the British Isles – or occasionally, at least, in exotic locations overseas.

I intend no sacrilege at all by saying that large numbers of such properties offer an illusion, at least, of some kind of secular heaven. Ancient manor houses and elegant former rectories set in handsome gardens and grounds vie with ultra-modern cliff-top residences or model farms and highland estates. More modest properties do exist admittedly yet what we gaze upon more often than not in the pages of the magazine remain unattainable dreams for most of us despite the vicarious pleasures of looking.

In days when I bought the publication regularly however, I began to notice a curious fact. That was how much the volume of the property advertising itself varied if not from month to month then at least from season to season.

Indeed it formerly puzzled me considerably why that should be so.

Yet the answer was basically very simple.

Apparently the volume of advertising peaks just before the nation's bankers receive their vast seasonal bonuses.

Rock musicians aside, such fiscal folk now seem almost the only ones who can afford the cream of Britain's rural retreats as these trickle slowly onto the market in all their magnificence. Pop celebrity Bob Geldof, for example, has lived for many years now in an ancient priory in Kent which once looked out upon a delightful cricket ground where my father and I both played at different times in our cricketing careers.

In total contrast, a friend still lives on a large English estate where members of his ancient Catholic family – the Welds – have been resident for more than 500 years. To the best of my belief he remains a thoroughly respected and well-liked landowner who even rebuilt the family castle which burned down in the 1920s.

Britain, however, is generally a very different country today from the one I left when I came to work in Australia twenty years ago. In some ways it has become largely unrecognizable, in fact, due largely to the global financial crisis but also to subsequently spiralling national debt.

Country life in Britain has always been a matter of complex historic customs and subtly interwoven social webs which are not always grasped fully by newcomers yet the priceless essential fabric continues somehow to endure.

Not only have the attitudes and often the general competence of those who govern Britain changed radically but so has the collective soul of the general populace due, in large part, to the recent global recession.

Do not the world's bankers bear some major responsibility for this?

In fact, a very general malaise exists today among most mature and aware citizens in Britain even though many might not find it easy to describe their symptoms precisely.

For my own part I felt much more generally confident in the world around me even during the twin decades from 1960 to 1980 when I was still trying, not very successfully, to make a living as a full-time artist. Yet I had the great privilege in those days of living in the beautiful and inexpensive surroundings of West Cornwall. In fact, the tall thin terraced house I bought in 1972 next door to the Catholic church in Penzance cost me only the equivalent of eighteen months even of my very limited earnings.

I sense no such housing bargains exist anywhere in Britain today.

Penzance in those days was a busy and prosperous market town which boasted a successful and large-scale deep-sea fishing industry from the adjacent port of Newlyn – which also somehow supported a well-known artists' colony from the late 19th century onwards. Today much of the look of prosperity has unfortunately vanished along with most of the fishing industry too – owing, in large part I understand, to the consequences of intrusive EU regulations.

The effects of the aftermath of the Global Financial Crisis in much of Britain are also particularly visible in other country towns I once knew well but which often look now close to dying on their feet. In suburban and metropolitan areas, however, the effects are rather less visible – in the South East of Britain at least.

Today Britons seem to exist very largely on debt to the extent that the prices of new cars are hard to find in the advertising put out by their manufacturers who now simply quote figures for monthly repayments instead.

Indeed all who lived what were once regarded as financially prudent lives here are now generally disadvantaged by a variety of factors such as an almost total lack of available interest on their savings, rapidly creeping inflation, devaluation of money because the government continues simply to print it – a predatory phenomenon known officially, if euphemistically, as 'quantitative easing'.

The entire financial nature of life in Britain, whether in the idyllic countryside or not, has thus become increasingly morally dishonest at its heart – as also has that of much of contemporary Europe.

Significantly, perhaps, what are known generally today as 'reflationary Keynesian measures' have their particular origins in the economic theories of prominent pre-war Bloomsbury socialite John Maynard Keynes who once described himself willingly as 'an immoralist'.

Indeed in a confession made to the Memoir Club in 1938, Keynes described himself and at least some of Bloomsbury's other former idols thus: "We were, that is to say, in the strict sense of the term, immoralists. The consequences of being found out had, of course, to be considered for what they were worth. But we recognized no moral obligation on us, no inner sanction, to conform or obey. Before heaven we claimed to be our own judge in our own case…It resulted in a general, widespread, though partly covert, suspicion affecting ourselves, our motives and our behaviour. It has deeply coloured the course of our lives in relation to the outside world. It is, I now think, a justifiable suspicion".

Ultimately I believe, Keynes saw the error of his ways and came to respect the extraordinary achievements of his predecessors in the ordering of British life and in the elaborate framework they devised to protect this order.

What some bankers have basically done in recent times to the world economy has effectively wrecked the lives of millions of conscientious people who have never erred themselves in their financial dealings. Sadly banks are almost as generally distrusted now in Europe as many of our politicians.

But are the suspicions so many of us hold still justified?

Forty years ago I luckily made the small amount of money I needed to convert the attic of my former house in Penzance into a working studio. I achieved this via a very modest transaction I made on the stock market.

Today, however, even such mild gambles are loaded so heavily against individuals rather than institutions that it would generally take a very intrepid investor indeed to achieve even such a minor result as mine. In any case, major investment banks now employ computerized robots to outwit and outspeed the rest of us in their stockmarket dealings. If recent memories of such divisive concepts as sub-prime mortgages and derivatives still disturb your rest at night, perhaps you are not ready yet for that of HFT – High Frequency Trading.

My favourite current rural village in England – in terms of its buildings, surroundings, pub, church and general ambience – is the little-known village of Lodsworth in Sussex which is about an hour's drive from where I presently live. The wonderful illustrator E.H.Shepard spent the last twenty years of his life there living comfortably, I hope, on the royalties he accrued from the memorable drawings he made for such children's classics as *Winnie the Pooh* and *Wind in the Willows*.

For me no one place or person represents more perfectly what British rural village life was once about.

Thankfully mere money did not mean everything in those days. Although it remains unseen, a morality attaches itself to transactions with money. Greed may surround itself with affluence yet in the long run ushers in the destruction of the delightfully complex structures of civilization itself.

Annals, June 2014

21

CHILD ABUSE OF A DIFFERENT KIND

Do you, too, find it strange how incidents of little apparent consequence lodge in the mind sometimes and subsequently set in train all sorts of serious reflections?

Roughly a decade ago a friend told me how deeply shocked he was when his six year old son came home from his primary school – situated in the Blue Mountains of New South Wales – and asked him "Why won't that horrid Mr.Howard say sorry to the Aborigines daddy?"

Clearly he was merely repeating what one of his teachers had said in his presence. Little children in local schools I visited at roughly the same time were often to be found hard at work making lurid 'global warming' posters years before learning even the rudiments of any kind of science themselves.

The father in question was angered especially I am sure because he was a Liberal voter yet the social and moral implications of the matter seem to me to go way beyond the matter of political allegiances.

To my mind, at least, it would be every bit as wrong if a small child were to come home from school and ask some very uncomplimentary question about a major ALP or Green Party political figure. But can you seriously imagine something of that kind happening in Australia?

And if you are unable to do that why exactly is that so?

We have long reached a stage I believe both in Australia and Britain where the political allegiances of a majority of teachers working in the public sector can be taken pretty much for granted.

Indeed more than two decades ago, before I had even set foot in Australia, I attended – in the company of a friend who was an Inspector of Schools – a giant farewell party thrown for all the teachers of Inner London Education Authority schools to mark the occasion of that body's final dissolution via a directive from Margaret Thatcher. Unsurprisingly the entertainments put on for the evening were very hostile indeed towards the latter. If she had appeared in person I believe she would undoubtedly have been physically attacked.

The question we need to ask ourselves here is why the children of literally millions of parents situated in Britain's largest city should be taught very largely by people who were overwhelmingly hostile to the elected national government of that time?

Margaret Thatcher was well aware that the former Inner London Education Authority provided a front behind which all sorts of radical Left initiatives and teaching took place – of which instruction in so-called 'Peace Studies' was merely one example.

When the preliminary work on devising a National Curriculum for English and Welsh schools took place in 1990-91 it was widely believed that my appointment to serve on one of the Working Groups was personally requested by Margaret Thatcher in the vain hope of redressing, however slightly, the predictable political bias of our group. In a sense I was easy to identify because I had already served for some years as visual arts spokesman on the government's Conservative Advisory Committee for the Arts and Heritage.

Equally easy to identify politically perhaps was the then Education Officer for one of Britain's major public galleries. His political affiliations certainly seemed in little doubt when in response to the suggestion I made to my Working Group that children even in our primary schools might begin to learn just a little bit about Britain's artistic heritage, he insisted that they must be simultaneously taught 'a Marxist version' of art history as well.

The so-called 'collapse of communism' in USSR and Eastern Europe was by then reasonably well advanced but so doctrinaire was the latter figure that it might as well have been Lenin himself rather than a Conservative government which had by then held power in

Britain for the previous decade.

To the best of my belief neither the Communist parties of Australia nor of Britain ever achieved more than a tiny fraction of the vote in national elections held in either country yet for decades Marxist influence pervaded British and Australian trades unions as just one direct consequence of which Britain is virtually without viable heavy industries today. In academia the pervasiveness of Marxist influence was certainly no less strong or virulent – as I pointed out more or less politely in last month's *Annals*.

Why the latter has been permitted to occur so widely is one of the more intriguing mysteries of our time.

Both Lenin and Marx, of course, held Christianity in utter contempt and in the case of the former personally ordered the murder of thousands of priests and other religious figures among other mass slaughters which he initiated.

In fact the phrase "religion is the opium of the people", which is widely attributed to Marx, had its true origins elsewhere but no serious doubt can be raised either about the latter's extreme hostility to Christian beliefs and teaching.

It can be argued I agree that Marx's purest venom was reserved for capitalism rather than Christianity yet today many forget that Marx died 130 years ago now. What did he know of modern trading conditions? The sixty four years of his life spanned the middle years of the 19th century and it is only the belief of his followers that he formulated what amounted to some kind of science that continues to bless his often grossly illogical philosophical theorising today with the least pretence of continuing relevance.

Like banking, capitalism as a whole requires an ethical umbrella as well as strict regulation if it is to function efficiently and productively for the common good.

If most of the bankers of the Western world had conducted their working lives recently by well-known Christian principles the world economy would now be in a completely different and infinitely better state.

At one time notable British banks made a point of recruiting their future management staff from private boarding schools similar to the one I attended myself where Christian values – such as fiscal and other forms of honesty – were encouraged at one time very vigorously indeed.

The whole business of education is certainly one of the major keys to the political futures of Australia and Britain – and to the viability of their economic futures also.

Tragically at the same-time that the increasing Left-wing politicisation of primary, secondary and tertiary education has taken place, standards of basic knowledge and ability – including literacy and numeracy – have generally fallen in spite of regular protestations to the contrary from the more powerful of the teaching unions.

Fear of tackling such unions head-on has deterred all but the most resolute politicians from facing up to such problems which are very well understood nonetheless by most responsible parents with children of school age.

Clearly, under the proper processes of democracy, teachers at any level must be and of course are at liberty to vote for any political party they choose.

What they should not be free to do, however, is indoctrinate the little children or effectively brainwash the young adults in their care with their own particular political attitudes and beliefs – yet the temptation to do so seems for some while to have been way beyond the capacities of most to resist.

That is because a great many share a kind of inbuilt, unreflective form of self-righteousness which some may find typical also of institutions such as the ABC – or of the BBC in Britain. Such people are often so certain of their rightness in every respect, in fact, as to be blindly intolerant of views which deviate in any way from their own.

I am sure we all remember here the comments made by a noted Australian academic following one of the federal re-elections of the Howard government to the effect that he and his colleagues must clearly have failed in their mission for such a political catastrophe to occur.

Perhaps I should mention here that my own father – who, for the earlier part of his career, at least, was what was known in pre-politically correct days as a schoolmaster – was a Labour voter in the first election to be held in Britain following the Second World War – the election which removed wartime leader Winston Churchill from power.

By some odd chance Churchill's political constituency included my boarding school but at the time of my leaving that institution at the end of seven years I had no idea at all about the political inclinations of any one of the excellent teachers the school employed.

To my mind, at least, that was absolutely as it should have been.

The aim to use education and the arts as highly promising areas for political indoctrination did not really get under way properly until the late 1960s – some years after I had left school. The so-called 'culture wars' also had their origins at that time as did the host of Marxist-inspired initiatives which came together over time to form the phenomenon known today as post-modernism.

In a recent survey I saw, a very high percentage of Green voters in Australia seemed to spring from the lowest age group of voters – in other words from those who had left school or university most recently.

In view of the degree of indoctrination which takes place regularly today in public education today why should any of us be surprised?

In Britain what amounts to a revolt has taken place in recent years against the kind of teaching regularly on offer in state secondary schools. Among other matters, the proposed replacement schools give parents an increased say in the way their children are taught.

In the coming weeks I hope to arrange meetings with some of those principally involved in these overdue and very welcome-seeming initiatives and will certainly report my full findings at a future time.

Australia is in a unique position at this moment not just to tidy up some of the mistakes made in its immediate past but to set an example to the world at large through the clarity, honesty and commonsense of fresh policies.

A major reappraisal of the way the arts and education are approached could be of general rather than minority benefit and also set a very desirable example for other Western countries to follow.

Annals, September 2013

22

THE TRIVIALISATION OF TRUTH

A dozen or so years ago while in the course of giving a talk at the University of Sydney I learned that my appointment there was due to be followed later that day by an address at Sydney Town Hall which would be given by someone infinitely more admired and respected than I within Australian academic circles: Jacques Derrida. The University of Sydney had, in fact, block-booked all the seats available for his lecture. Mass adulation was clearly the order of the day.

By some odd chance my wife and I were employing an extraordinarily erudite and widely-read house painter at that time. The following day I asked him how much work by Derrida he had ever read.

When he replied " around one hundred and twenty pages" I was quick to compliment him.

But he was equally quick to disillusion me.

"In fact I read the same four pages thirty times while trying to extract any kind of intelligible meaning from them" he informed me ashamedly.

I am sure we all remember the word 'deconstruction' – the convoluted academic exercise of the day closely associated with Derrida's name.

It was a technique, in fact, which caused someone I know – who was formerly a senior teacher of English at a pleasant school in outer London – to take early retirement from her career when she was ordered to instruct her students in its mysteries. When not so instructed she was a passionate advocate of the continuing relevance of Shakespeare to everyday modern life.

Did any way exist at the time in which she could have shown herself to be more academically unfashionable?

The so-called 'culture wars' certainly had – and probably continue to have – their fair share of victims as well as beneficiaries. But the greatest victim by far of the academic era which began in the 1980s – when words such as deconstruction and structuralism along with the novel vocabulary which supported their apparent imperatives were still very much in vogue – was the fundamental concept of truth itself.

It may seem obvious to us here that the entire concept of truth is intrinsic not just to religious belief, say, or to the traditional discipline of philosophy but also to the ordered workings of society itself.

Without a fundamental notion of the importance of truth societies tend to mutate – with potentially disastrous consequences – as the all too recent examples of a fascist Nazi Germany and a communist USSR might suggest.

Both power-obsessed and rigidly enforced systems would have been inconceivable, of course, without the philosophic and political underpinnings of Friedrich Nietzsche and Karl Marx respectively, however much their supporters may claim that the fundamental natures of the doctrines of both were misunderstood at least in part.

In the godless world or godless political system that Nietzsche and Marx did so much to promote the notion that absolute truth might exist at all soon came to find itself regarded as intellectually absurd.

If there is to be no after-life, of course, then the entire notion of absolute truth – which might subject our lives at some point to its inconvenient scrutiny – may indeed come to seem happily superfluous.

At the height of the era when deconstruction and structuralism formed the daily stuff of academic discourse – and before these were supplanted in turn by other neo-Marxist hybrids such as cultural, post-colonial and gender studies, queer theory or the politics of grievance – I was approached by a young woman at an art gallery who asked for my assistance in interpreting some of the works on view.

At the end of twenty minutes of earnest effort she was kind

enough to thank me cordially while remarking at the same time that what I had said was "only *your* truth, of course".

Because I had not been teaching in tertiary institutions for some while her words were the first evidence I had heard that truth and opinion had suddenly become synonymous – and even interchangeable somehow – in the fashionable academic parlance of such places.

I even asked her politely what exactly she had meant.

Her slightly garbled reply involved a somewhat extreme form of determinism: my 'truths', in short, were apparently predetermined entirely by my gender, background, ethnicity, education, age – and even height. But if I had been short, black, female, underprivileged and thirty years younger my 'truths' would thus inevitably have been quite different.

In the past forty years the humanities departments of Western universities – which were once guardians of our moral as well as academic traditions have generally fallen over themselves in a fashion-conscious rush to betray both traditions.

Two writers in particular stand out here for the consistency of their opposition to those who have effectively betrayed the great traditions of Western academic life: the English philosopher Roger Scruton and the noted American writer and journalist Roger Kimball.

The words that follow form the first paragraph of the section devoted by Scruton to deconstruction in his book *Modern Philosophy* (Arrow Books 1997). These words also certainly go a long way to explaining the adulation received by Jacques Derrida as the sometime guest of the University of Sydney:

> "By demonstrating that all law and interdiction, all meaning and value, all that troubles, contains or limits us, is our own invention, the devil fosters the belief that everything is permitted. In particular, revenge is permitted against the society from which you feel excluded and against the Father who created it. If you have reached the stage of repudiation, and are unable to advance beyond it to the reconciliation and forgiveness which are the signs

of moral maturity, then the temptation of the liberator is irresistible. 'Ruin the sacred truths' as Marvell said; pull down the order that surrounds you; not only do you affirm yourself against it, you also liberate your fellows and will be rewarded by their admiring love".

Here is Kimball on the same subject – an extract from his *Experiments against Reality* (Ivan R.Dee, Chicago 2000): "But because deconstruction operates by subversion, its evasions are at the same time an attack: an attack on the cogency of language and the moral and intellectual claims that language has codified in tradition. The subversive element inherent in the deconstructive enterprise is another reason that it has exercised such a mesmerizing spell on intellectuals eager to demonstrate their radical *bona fides*. Because it attacks the intellectual foundations of the established order, deconstruction promises its adherents not only an emancipation from the responsibilities of truth but also the prospect of engaging in a species of radical activism. A blow against the legitimacy of language, they imagine, is at the same time a blow against the legitimacy of the tradition in which language lives and has meaning. They are not mistaken about this. For it is by undercutting the idea of truth that the deconstructionist also undercuts the idea of value, including social, moral and political values".

Although they often seem to be at one remove, at least, from the normal activities of the community, Western universities continue to initiate notions which flow out at varying speeds into the wider and less privileged world that surrounds them.

Thus – without necessarily realising this – the community slowly absorbs all sorts of ideas which seem, at first sight, to have little or no relevance to everyday life. Indeed, virtually all of the concepts which are marshalled today under the collective banner of post-modernism slowly infiltrated the general consciousness in precisely this fashion.

It would indeed be very hard to imagine political correctness, say, erupting spontaneously as an idea in the Western suburbs of Sydney.

Instead the basic notion of political correctness wafted gently across the Pacific all the way from the ivory towers of the University of California at Berkeley. Multiculturalism, feminism and so-called gender issues also, for example, first took root likewise in other quarters of our globe yet nevertheless seem by now to have embedded themselves inextricably in Australian life.

Understandably the prevailing mood of universities during the heydays of deconstruction and such soon became one of atheistic cynicism – which found itself described more politely by some people as 'irony' – but foreseeably this 'ironic' contagion then also spread out in time into the wider community.

If no truth does indeed exist outside human 'constructs' – as deconstruction and structuralism suggest – then surely the acquisition of money, power and self-gratification by any means possible becomes even more attractive to all who lack basic moral strength.

In a world proved to the satisfaction of so many to be 'godless' why should we not all surrender ourselves to outright avarice, say, or a lust for power?

To my mind Western universities in recent times have generally betrayed the trust once placed in them by ordinary people – the children of a good many of whom will have been practising Christians of course.

Why should they too be instructed in godlessness?

The world in which I grew up was one in which secularised Christianity retained a primary influence in the affairs of individuals as well as of nations and where the examples of great art and great literature still set a model which was untainted as yet by cynicism. Politicians still existed who even put the needs of their nations before their own.

Why has that world been replaced by now by one which is infinitely less attractive and in which young supposedly educated adults cannot even grasp the fundamental difference between truth and opinion?

I fear the increasing politicisation of education in the West at all levels has played a preponderant part.

Annals, August 2013

23

NEVER TOO LATE TO LEARN

Some years ago an advertisement for an insurance company – if I remember correctly – ran the following witty if somewhat ominous-seeming headline: THREE SCORE YEARS AND THEN?

For those of us who have managed to creep, at least, past the formerly prescribed milestone of seventy a temptation exists, understandably enough, to imagine – in the words of a popular expression – that we have 'seen it all'.

In terms of delightful, encouraging and engaging events the latter might indeed be a fairly accurate summary of my sentiments. In terms of negative experiences, however, I realise increasingly now that I may be a mere novice.

For instance, fifteen months after returning to the country which I regarded for much of my life as 'home' I find myself awaiting each day's new newspaper headlines with trepidation rather than the least expectation of pleasure.

Try this headline, for example, culled from the 16 March edition of *The Daily Telegraph*, Britain's most sober and reasonable newspaper: MANIPULATING DEATH RATES TO BE MADE ILLEGAL.

The first two paragraphs of the story ran as follows: "A new criminal offence to stop NHS (National Health Service) hospitals 'fiddling' official figures is to be introduced by ministers in the wake of the Mid Staffordshire scandal. Jeremy Hunt, the Health Secretary, is to announce that senior NHS managers and hospital trusts will be made criminally liable if they manipulate figures on waiting times and death rates".

Let me explain this sombre little tale a bit further. In recent weeks it has emerged in Britain that up to 1,200 patients died quite unnecessarily in Mid Staffordshire hospitals in recent years as a direct result of what is euphemistically described as 'poor care' and that similarly depressing figures seem to exist elsewhere also now in our formerly admirable NHS hospitals.

As in many other Western countries, including Australia, the number of people classified as elderly as a percentage of the total population has increased steadily in Britain. Indeed pensions for the elderly here account now for roughly half of this nation's already overstretched welfare budget.

While I therefore agree that the fact that senior health managers have tried to conceal large numbers of 'unnecessary' deaths is deeply shocking what is more alarming still to me is a strong suspicion that keeping large numbers of frail and elderly people alive 'unnecessarily' may now be frowned upon secretly somewhere else in our 'official circles'. Finding the correct people to blame for 'unnecessary' deaths thus strikes me as only one part of a problem based on secretive policies.

What, if anything at all, does the expression 'the Liverpool care pathway' mean to you? My guess is probably nothing.

Indeed until returning to Britain late in 2011, I, too, had never heard of 'the Liverpool care pathway' but now know it to be a procedure borrowed apparently from thoroughly reputable hospices for allowing the terminally ill to die with dignity through the withdrawal of essential, life-sustaining services.

Supposedly this procedure can take place only with the full consent of patients themselves and of their nearest and dearest but regrettably that has not turned out to be by any means invariably the case. One also cannot help wondering here who precisely decides whether or not patients are 'terminally ill' in the first place?

Most worryingly of all, however, attractive incentives apparently exist or have existed for NHS hospitals to include the so-called 'Liverpool pathway' in their procedures.

Might this be an effective beginning, in fact, of 'euthanasia by the back door'?

In Britain the existence of a punitive inheritance tax might also seem something of a disincentive in any national struggle to prolong the lives of the elderly by all means possible.

As I have suggested already there now still seems rather a lot to learn in Britain whatever one's age.

In the past few years, for example, we have become obliged to learn that our banks are not automatic models of probity or good sense but were co-conspirators instead in the selling of toxic, derivative bonds which have contributed at least their fair share to the creation of the Western world's current, seemingly insoluble economic crisis.

In Britain, many also believe that former Chancellor and Prime Minister Gordon Brown effectively 'booby-trapped' our economy after years of profligate spending so that an incoming conservative government would face a Herculean if not impossible task. Did he have no feelings at all for the effect of such an action on ordinary people?

As an artist and writer brought up in the English countryside, the outstanding beauty of much of rural England has always seemed to me a most vital part of our national heritage.

However, because of an agreement made by a previous government Britain is obliged now to cut 'carbon emissions' by a staggering four fifths in less than 40 years.

Already parts of the English countryside with which I have long been familiar are becoming immersed by acres of solar panels which conceal what was once fertile farmland.

During the past fifteen months, however, the sun has scarcely appeared at all in Britain so that such panels seem even less likely to contribute to our future power needs than the gigantic wind turbines which threaten to blight even the most famous parts of our land. A future Thomas Hardy might thus be obliged now to write rural novels such as *Far from the Madding Solar Panels* or a contemporary John Constable to create *The Hay Wain with Local Wind Turbine 2021* – some 200 years, in fact, after the original event.

Nobody knows where the next outcrop of such excrescences will appear so that all hopes for some future rural idyll in England are by now effectively placed on hold.

Even thirty years ago no-one would have believed such a scenario was even remotely possible but we seem to live now in an age of collective madness wherein no act of future folly can be discounted entirely.

Based simply on the empirical evidence of the past 15 months the onset of a minor ice age certainly seems no less likely to me at present than significant global warming. On the third day of spring here our entire country is being swept by blizzards in a manner which has not occurred here for the past 50 years.

As regular readers of *Annals* will know I have been a 'climate change sceptic' for years not least because of the decades of experience I have had in identifying the distinctive timbre of spurious arguments whether these concern art, literature, education or so-called 'global warming'.

If you read no other part of his long and convincingly argued book at least read chapter 8, the concluding chapter of Ian Plimer's *Heaven & Earth* (Connor Court 2009) and take to heart what it says.

In this 500 page book Professor Plimer, one of Australia's more eminent scientists, argues that no legitimate scientific link has ever been established between man-made carbon dioxide emissions and so-called climate change. He does so calmly and convincingly and without any of the now customary hysteria which attends this subject.

> Here is the first paragraph of his chapter 8: "We are facing the greatest global threat in my three score and two years. It is not from global warming. It is the threat from policy responses to perceived global warming and the demonising of dissent. These policies also threaten freedoms and the nature of science and religion. Policy changes have the ability to reduce base load energy supplies of electricity that underpin employment and the standard of living".

Unfortunately we seem to live now in an age of calamitous

decisions – often foisted on us by authorities who should know better. Ideology is generally the key to their madness – as in the recent case of the Euro – plus an overwhelming, totalitarian desire to tell the rest of us what to do.

Back in 1990-91, I spent eighteen months serving on one of the working groups for the National Curriculum for English and Welsh schools and was regularly astonished by the effects ideology seemed to have on some of my colleagues one of whom seriously proposed teaching a Marxist version of art history to our nation's six year olds.

Perhaps the brightest light of the past depressing week has been cast by an article by former colleague Harry Mount (*The Daily Telegraph* 21 March) who patiently explained to 100 of modern Britain's academics why children can't think if they don't learn facts.

I reproduce the first paragraph of his article solely so that I can end on a high note: "When future generations come to study the causes of Britain's global decline, Exhibit A will be a letter in yesterday's *Daily Telegraph* signed by 100 academics from across the country. In it, the various professors attacked Michael Gove's proposed national curriculum for consisting of 'endless lists of spellings, facts and rules". My God, the madness! Sometimes the Education Secretary must wake up in the morning and wonder whether it's all worth the struggle. His opponents are of such a deep strain of perverse idiocy that it is impossible to argue with them – ideology has totally defeated reason".

To which I can but add "Amen".

Annals, April 2013

24

FORTUNATE LIVES

During an address I was asked to give at a funeral last year I referred to a book I unearthed many years ago in a second-hand bookshop.

The book in question – which I can no longer locate – was called *Ask the fellows who cut the hay* and the point I tried to make at the funeral was how much we can all learn from listening to the reminiscences of elderly people – such as those of the recently deceased.

Ask the fellows who cut the hay was, in fact, an attempt made many years ago to place on record an oral history of farmworkers in Britain for as far back as anyone could remember. It also included the memories passed on from the parents and grandparents of those interviewed for the book.

My purpose in recalling the book now relates to the relative austerity which apparently faces much of the developed world – an austerity to which few people are any longer accustomed.

By contrast, farmworkers in 19th century Britain were thoroughly accustomed to lives with a degree of austerity and lack of material possessions which are hard to imagine today yet, if their recollections are to be believed, many were apparently not just stoical but actively happy about their lives.

Their diet consisted almost entirely, so far as I can recall, of home-baked bread and home-brewed beer – both of which were highly nutritious – supplemented by occasional vegetables and rabbits and, more occasionally still, by pork. Most kept a pig of their own on small allocations of land.

Self-evidently artificial entertainment and consumer goods did not feature at all in their lives. But thrift, 'making-do', neighbourly kindness and demanding physical toil all unquestionably did.

One of the reasons why I found *Ask the fellows who cut the hay* especially intriguing is that I grew up in the English countryside myself.

When I was little, draught horses were still in regular use for ploughing and hauling carts, a circumstance which may have been prolonged artificially because fuel of any kind – along with much else – was in very short supply in Britain during the Second World War.

Because our family home lay in a direct path of possible invasion my sister and I were evacuated twice.

When we finally returned home our Kentish garden provided us with a grandstand view of aerial combats during the day and welcome refuge – via a simple dug-out air-raid shelter – at night.

Small children tend to be innocent and unknowing admittedly but most of my memories from this phase of my life are extremely happy ones.

Most of the credit for that is undoubtedly due to the calm and fortitude displayed by my parents.

My mother, in particular, already had plenty of experience of the possible consequences of war since two of her three brothers of military age – along with the man to whom she was then engaged – were killed in the First World War, while her third brother was seriously wounded.

During noisy, nocturnal air-raids my father read to us tirelessly by torchlight. The only book I now recollect him reading was *Children of the New Forest* and his rendition of this shortly – and happily – encouraged in me a voracious appetite for reading myself, a habit I have never relinquished.

In the absence of fuel, all of us travelled almost everywhere by bicycle.

Since holidays away from home were not a wartime option, we varied our individual daily routes as much as we could and also went on day outings and picnics regularly as a family.

Usually such outdoor destinations were chosen for particular features such as the presence of interesting wildflowers or wildlife or, in one instance, for its outcrops of chalk from blocks of which we carved attempted sculptural portraits of each other with the penknives most males carried in those days.

My father had a particular knack of inducing nightingales to sing by skilfully imitating their warm-up notes. All of us shared an equally passionate interest in natural history.

On days when outdoor activities were impossible and my sister and I were not at school my mother, who was a good amateur artist herself, set us – and occasional visiting cousins – highly demanding subjects for drawing.

Since food was scarce – and rationed anyway – and TV non-existent at the time none of us stood much danger of becoming inactive let alone obese. My own particular obsessions of the time centred around playing tennis and climbing trees so that I was generally exhausted by nightfall.

Neither of my parents were regular church-goers – my own interest in Christianity occurred later in life – but from my memories of them and of scores of rural people like them I have some clue at least of why, from the most unpromising circumstances, Britain finally emerged on the winning side in the Second World War.

If exactly the same circumstances were replicated today – but involving instead the present-day inhabitants of Britain – I do not think the country as a whole would perform nearly as well. Something deleterious has happened, in fact, while no-one was looking, to the collective moral fibre of much of the developed world.

While some small part of the blame for this could be attributed to politicians whose increasing employment of 'spin' encourages widespread cynicism among the electorate and another slice might be laid at the door of the media which, with few honourable exceptions such as this journal, dumbs down or brutalises just about everything it touches, I see the major cause of the developed world's decline as post-modernist theory and the armies of so-called educators who skilfully implant its generally pernicious precepts into the innocent heads of our young.

I have said already how fortunate I think my childhood was compared with that of most of today's children.

Among its more obvious advantages were a total absence of television and its brain-numbing children's programmes, computer games, fast food and mobile telephones.

Yet less evident advantages were possibly even more important. Among these were the belief – widely laughed at today – that truth in the singular really does exist, that objectivity is not only possible but desirable and that most great reputations gained in the arts and letters were very generally deserved.

Much of the fabric of Western civilisation was indeed founded on the genius and extraordinary efforts of dead white European males – the DWEMs derided so regularly today by feminists.

Might January 2009 be as good a time as any to start remembering at least some of the rocks on which civilisation itself was founded?

Annals, January/February 2009

25

WHY INJUSTICE IS AN ARGUMENT FOR AN AFTER-LIFE

In recent articles about atheism, a number of experienced commentators seemed to me, at least, to get hold of completely the wrong end of the stick.

In short they categorised atheism as though it were an alternative system of belief rather than one simply of disbelief.

Thus when Julia Gillard, for example, presents herself as an atheist all that really tells us about her – if you think about it even for a moment – is what she does *not* believe.

Indeed, disbelief in God apart, atheists everywhere presumably feel themselves at liberty to believe in absolutely anything at all from polygamy, say, to UFOs.

It would thus be extremely unlikely, in statistical terms, to find any two atheists anywhere who hold an identical set of *beliefs*.

In contrast to a figure such as the current leader of the opposition, Mr.Abbott, whose known Catholicism usefully tells us a great deal about him and what he believes, Gillard's atheism tells us, for certain, only a single thing about her: that she doesn't apparently – for the moment at least – believe in any God.

To be fair to her, Gillard's political enthusiasms could be held to add up to some kind of social moral code which occasionally, at least, may run parallel to Christian notions of virtue.

Before the advent of post-modernism, of course, most of what were deemed moral or social virtues in Western countries were Christian in origin.

However, unlike atheism post-modern precepts – when assembled together – really do represent an alternative as well as extremely insidious orthodoxy of thought.

Thus while avowed atheists might feel under no obligation at all to support same-sex marriages, say, or so-called multiculturalism, both of the latter represent veritable cornerstones of post-modernist orthodoxy.

Atheism may be a prevalent component of post-modernism yet is not necessarily a compulsory one. Indeed, it is only when all the components of post-modernism are put together that the whole emerges evidently as neo-Marxist – and often virulently anti-Christian – in nature.

In accordance with the basic Marxist concept of *Realpolitik*, post-modernism supplants notions of justice with those of power. Thus post-modernist initiatives such as political correctness do not seek to impose themselves on us today through a wide sharing of beliefs but often through the compulsions of social legislation.

In Britain some years ago, for example, when it became well-known and established that a very high percentage of street muggings in London were carried out by persons of Afro-Caribbean origin it was made illegal to say or even imply so under anti-discriminatory laws.

In the meantime the facts were at least as well known to the Metropolitan Commissioner of Police as to the proverbial man on the Clapham omnibus. The novel laws of anti-discrimination thus opposed not only justice but the purposes of law-enforcement which are framed to serve a common good.

Atheists often say that they cannot believe in a God who allows disasters to happen or apparent human horrors or injustices to take place.

Here they are often ignorant of or fail to understand the doctrine of free will which really ought not to tax any intelligent person's powers of comprehension.

However, I personally believe conversely that horrors such as the Holocaust present a very strong argument indeed for the existence of an after-life. How can one possibly believe in justice and not believe that to be so?

To put the matter simply, how can one believe that the brutally curtailed lives of gassed children can possibly represent the culmination of any story?

To me, such a thought is intolerable.

For justice to exist, there must be both an after-life for such innocent children and a continuation of the story which involves just punishment for their oppressors.

I do not come from a practising Christian family but can at least sympathise with my mother, who lost two of her three brothers of military age and the man to whom she was then engaged in the First World War. Her third brother narrowly escaped death at Pozieres but lost a lung. My mother's religious faith was also unfortunately – but perhaps understandably – a victim of that conflict.

Today few young people I know in England or Australia have ever been forced to confront such losses and many, in consequence, pay little heed to many of the major issues of human life.

My mother belonged nevertheless to a world in which consideration for other people and the existence of a basic moral code were still very much the norm.

What directly underwrote such civilising tendencies were the continuing importance of family groups and of their close social interaction. Atheism and humanism may have attracted growing numbers of people even back then yet Christian principles still provided the bedrock of most public life. Indeed, until about 40 years ago this continued to be the case in most Western countries.

40 years ago, however, those of us who were alive at the time witnessed the advent of the so-called 'cultural revolution' in Western countries. Yet the description of that revolution as 'cultural' is in a sense misleading unless we accept that adjective in its broadest sense.

One unfortunate consequence is that the whole concept of a 'cultural' revolution sounds relatively harmless, as though the whole affair took place behind the closed doors of academic institutions and had minimal effect on ordinary people or their lives.

No greater delusion could exist because by now the various strands of post-modernist ideology have combined to transform almost every aspect of daily life.

For example, would the notion of adoptions by same-sex couples have been considered as even a remote possibility 40 years ago?

Yet within the past few weeks the legality of such adoptions passed into law in New South Wales with an absolute minimum of public comment.

When stage-hands shift scenery in theatres the lights which illuminate the stage are generally extinguished so that a desired transition appears to take place seamlessly.

Who said "The condition upon which God hath given liberty to man is eternal vigilance"?

Few by now will remember the name of the author but, worse still, society at large has forgotten the continued cogency of his message.

It is to the enduring shame of Western society that it has been effectively transformed while far too many of us were asleep.

Annals, October 2010

26

A SHORT HISTORY OF INADEQUATE THINKING

As years pass by I find it becomes increasingly easy to forget not just episodes but quite significant periods of my life; this whole issue has arisen, in fact, because I have been working for some time on a book of memoirs.

Just one such largely forgotten period was a spell of four years duration spent teaching art history to aspiring painters at an art school in the South of England.

In doing this I tried hard to make the past come alive in the minds of my students and to combat a notion widely held at that time – the early 1980s – that art history was somehow a boring and unnecessary adjunct to the seriously relevant task of being a contemporary painter.

Of what conceivable consequence, the intensely revolutionary young artist might demand, could even a famous 17th century painting such as *The Surrender of Breda* (1634-35) by Diego Velazquez be for any dedicated young modernist?

What possible interest could an image of a military surrender conducted by soldiers armed with swords and pikes have in an age of supersonic jet aircraft and laser-guided missiles?

The somewhat inconvenient fact I remember pointing out at the time was that in spite of our admitted wonders of technological advance nobody had subsequently painted with greater intelligence, understanding or sublime levels of skill than the 17th century Spanish master who lived and worked in those distant-seeming days between 1599 and 1661.

Indeed much the same argument could be applied also to two other absolute masters active in the first three quarters of the 17th century: Rembrandt van Rijn (1606-69) and Jan Vermeer (1632-75).

Why then – by common consent among those who properly understand the matter – has not painting 'progressed' qualitatively and seemingly inevitably in precisely the same manner as technology and science?

I do not suggest here that the subsequent 18th, 19th and 20th centuries did not produce artists of exceptional merit – although the 18th century was perhaps a time more noted for great music than for great visual art – but continue to aver than none of these possessed the superhuman levels of painterly skill demonstrated time and again by Velazquez. Indeed, supreme artists of the 19th and 20th centuries such as Edouard Manet (1832-83) and Pablo Picasso (1881-1973) would have been among the first to acknowledge that fact.

Interestingly, the rigorous artistic training undergone by Velazquez would surely be looked on as unacceptable or even cruel today – he was apprenticed to the painter Pacheco at the age of 11 and became an acknowledged master of his craft at the age of 17 with his induction into the Guild of St.Luke. Nor was his general education by any means neglected in spite of the long hours he spent in Pacheco's studio.

Why, then, do we no longer train artists of precocious talent in such a rigorous way when we train top young players of musical instruments – and even top tennis juniors – in such a demanding manner from even earlier ages?

One of the more irritating heresies of the modern age is that 'progress' is inevitable in just about every discipline and sphere – not least, perhaps, in matters of religious faith.

I suggest here that 'progress' and 'progressive' are words used much too readily in a purely rhetorical way when what is being described is often, in reality, absolutely nothing of the kind.

For instance, if the major tenets of the Catholic faith are and always were true – not least through being divinely inspired – then surely they don't need meddling with now or at any time in the future in the name of 'progress' or of anything else.

In short, what is true remains true. In the words of the famous Australian idiom, in fact, "if it aint broke don't fix it".

Sadly words such as the foregoing are automatically anathema to proponents of novelty and non-stop revolution.

It is also worth mentioning here, however, that the history of Western art provides another intriguing parallel with that of the Christian faith.

While Western visual art from the time of Giotto di Bondone (1267-1337) preoccupied itself largely with perceptual appearance *a central, continuous spine remained apparent at the heart of artistic practice.*

Giotto is regarded, in fact, as the founder of the central tradition of Western painting precisely because his work broke free from the stylisations of Byzantine and other early Christian art by introducing a new ideal of naturalism – truth to natural appearances – plus a convincing sense of pictorial space. This process continued just as markedly during the Renaissance which dated from the late 14th to the late 16th centuries.

Admittedly, small numbers of movements which deviated from this central spinal thrust occurred – such as Mannerism which lasted roughly from the time of the High Renaissance to the beginning of the Baroque – but often these were relatively short-lived.

Purely for alliterative convenience we could characterise the period when the central, spinal trait of realism remained dominant in Western art as being from the time of the beginning of Giotto's inspired practice – about 1300 – to the death of Gauguin in 1903. For roughly six centuries, in short – from the time of Giotto to Gauguin – the number of readily identifiable artistic movements remained relatively small.

But from the moment that the great schism of modern art with the past took place both observably and philosophically – which I would date for convenience from the first exhibition of Fauve art in 1906 – the fractured body of Western painting began to split continuously into a host of new movements. During the whole of the 20th century, in fact, there was at least one readily identifiable new modern or post-modern art movement for every two and a half years.

In short, from the time when a total split with the past was first thought desirable by 'modernists', the schismatic body could not agree at all about the new forms such a break with the past should take *other than that novelty must always replace continuity*.

Do you detect some parallel here with the course taken within Christianity by the schismatic body of the church since the time of the Reformation?

I would be disappointed if you did not.

Following the initial fracture in the cases both of art and of the Christian religion, the schismatic body fractures and refractures to the extent that what is ultimately left at times becomes unrecognisable either as art or as Christianity.

A sorry state indeed.

Annals, September 2011

27

TRUE HISTORY, FALSE ARGUMENTS

Recently I was lucky enough to spend a few nights with old friends in the ancient city of Norwich. I had been best man at my host's wedding there more than 40 years ago.

Norwich, the main city of East Anglia on England's East Coast, boasts two cathedrals, more than thirty mediaeval churches and a centre so full of ancient, distinguished buildings that it comes almost as a shock to see people going about their daily business there clad in modern attire.

The first of the cathedrals, which dates originally from the 11th century, lost its spire twice and has been ravaged by fire three times yet stands magnificently today in its full glory in the middle of unusually gracious and extensive cathedral precincts.

Prior to the Reformation this was, of course, a Catholic cathedral as were all of the other Norman and Gothic cathedrals of England. Why do so many people forget this?

The second of the city's cathedrals, dedicated to St.John the Baptist, was begun as recently as 1882 and completed in 1910 but did not achieve its present status as a cathedral until 1976.

Before that it was merely one of the city's so-called Strangers' churches having been commissioned by the Catholic 15th Duke of Norfolk as a thank-offering to God following his very happy marriage.

All non-Anglican churches were known once upon a time in Norwich as Strangers' churches but this was, by some way, the most magnificent of them all. Ironically for a church conceived as a thank-offering it is situated in Norwich's lengthy but quaintly-named Unthank Road. George Unthank was formerly a prominent local builder.

It amuses me sometimes to reflect that the present-day population of Norwich is roughly the same as that of, say, the Australian town of Wollongong – or that of 16th century Venice and its surroundings. Yet back in 1750 Norwich was England's third highest centre of population, exceeded only by London and Bristol.

Today it has become much too common among people such as politicians to bless the mere passage of time with automatic but often misleading descriptions such as 'evolution' and 'progress'.

Therefore why, in theory at least, should not a modern town such as Wollongong be able to match the cultural, architectural and aesthetic achievements of similarly-sized 16th century Venice which produced not only some of the finest architecture – such as the library of San Marco by Jacopo Sansovino – but paintings by such as Giovanni Bellini, Giorgione, Veronese and Titian which have seldom been surpassed in the whole history of the world?

Clearly the passage of time by itself is no guarantee of anything at all.

It is equally evident that culture at the highest level is not dependent in any way simply on population – nor even on the wonders of modern technology. You may ask here how Sansovino could possibly have coped without a computer in forging the extreme intricacy of his buildings or Titian in running his Venetian life without even a motor boat to travel in or a state-of-the-art mobile phone to make appointments with his patrons?

It has become a recent fashion in Western countries such as Britain and Australia to attack Christian teaching on the grounds of its unforgivable antiquity – and thus of its supposed anachronism and irrelevance – in a manner which has probably never occurred before in the history of the Christian faith.

I am perhaps particularly aware of dishonest use of language and reasoning from the twenty-odd years during which I wrote art criticism for a living and when art which often lacked distinction of any kind was described regularly by my critical colleagues as 'progressive', 'evolutionary' or 'advanced'.

The formal trappings of art and literature do, of course, change and develop over time – but by no means invariably, let alone inevitably for the better.

On the other hand the teachings of Christ were never intended to be either merely 'evolutionary', 'works in progress' or some temporary, philosophic stop-gap. Nor were they ever treated as such in past centuries by any who professed themselves to be Christians. To put the matter simply, Christ's teachings were obviously intended to be for the permanent guidance of mankind and not merely until something 'better' turned up or until his guidance ceased to seem altogether convenient for the apparent exigencies of 'modern' life.

In such a precise context, it is appropriate perhaps to look for a moment at some of the contents of an advisory letter devised recently by senior members of the British cabinet for their conservative colleagues: "Civil partnerships for gay couples were a great step forward but the question now is whether it is any longer acceptable to exclude people from marriage simply because they love someone of the same sex. Marriage has evolved over time. We believe that opening it up to same-sex couples will strengthen, not weaken, the institution. Attitudes to gay people have changed. A substantial majority of the public now favour allowing same-sex couples to marry, and support has increased rapidly. This is the right thing to do at the right time."

Not only have the British people not yet been allowed their long-promised referendum regarding membership of the European Union but neither – to the best of my knowledge – has public opinion ever even been researched properly on the subject of same-sex marriage.

As an example of dishonestly-conceived argument much of the foregoing seems hard to improve upon.

Indeed, as recent voting figures have shown, less than half of Britain's current conservative MPs themselves support so-called gay marriage. Nevertheless, Chris Grayling, the government's Justice

Secretary has just backed proposed same-sex marriage legislation in the following words: "It is a sensible next step in the evolution of social attitudes."

Has the innocent word 'evolution' ever been used in a more dishonest or tendentious manner?

Indeed, might Mr. Grayling even have been tempted to use it in such fashion by the way the word is used so regularly and inappropriately in the arts?

That question seems worth asking.

In Australia it becomes all too easy for the populace to forget the momentous past achievements of humanity in the arts and architecture because so little evidence of this stares them daily in the face.

Thus even so fine an edifice as St. Mary's Cathedral in Sydney is still less than 100 years old in contrast to the 600 great Gothic cathedrals and churches of Europe – all of them once Catholic – most of which had been completed by the year 1300.

In cities such as Norwich visitors find themselves tapped on the shoulder by history for much of their time there.

In the surrounding, mostly flat countryside the towers of countless ancient churches appear suddenly from the surrounding fields like skyward pointing fingers to remind us of the role that Christ once played in the lives of humble farmers and shepherds, weavers and other tradesmen and their womenfolk. The former prosperity of the county of Norfolk was once based very firmly on the raising of sheep.

To this day Norfolk remains the driest and sunniest – if by no means the warmest – county in England.

To the North West of Norwich lies the famous village of Walsingham which has been a site of Catholic pilgrimage for approaching a thousand years. Indeed, the religious story of the village antedates even England's historically crucial Battle of Hastings. Some years ago, I was fortunate enough to stay with friends in the nearby, oddly-named village of Great Snoring.

It was in the year 1061 in fact that Richelis de Faverches prayed one night that she might undertake some special work in honour of Our Lady. In answer to her prayer, the Virgin Mary led her in spirit to Nazareth and showed her the precise place where the Annunciation had taken place. Tradition holds that she then asked her to build a replica in Walsingham as a permanent memorial.

The Augustinian Canons built a Priory at Walsingham c.1150, the village then going on to become one of the greatest shrines in mediaeval Christendom. This survived for nearly four hundred years until at the time of the Reformation the famous statue of Our Lady of Walsingham was taken to London and publicly burnt.

Often the history of England seems to me like that of a gnarled tree, twisted out of shape for all time by the darker days of the Reformation. No further pilgrimages took place openly at Walsingham again until 1829 when the Act of Catholic Emancipation at last allowed public expressions of Catholic faith to resume.

The 19th century had almost come to a close when a faithful person, Charlotte Pearson Boyd purchased the last of the wayside chapels en route to Walsingham and restored it for Catholic use. This 14th century building was known as the Slipper Chapel. 38 years later the site was visited by the Catholic bishops of England and Wales in the company of 10,000 pilgrims. Today, during the pilgrimage season, Walsingham attracts more than ten times that number of worshippers.

At times, England's ancient county of Norfolk can seem like an island of sanity in the growing madness and self-destructiveness of the modern world.

Annals, March 2013

<h1 style="text-align:center">28</h1>

A FILM ALMOST EVERYONE MISSED

I wonder how many of you saw the 1944 black and white film *A Canterbury Tale* when it was screened at 3p.m. last Saturday on ABC1 TV? That particular time coincided, of course, with the screening on a different channel of the AFL Cup Final.

The great many who will thus have automatically missed the film deprived themselves of an extraordinary and haunting experience which was rendered especially poignant for me, at least, because it dealt with both the era and immediate physical surroundings of my Kentish childhood.

Canterbury cathedral was, as some may still know, the scene of the murder of Archbishop Thomas a Becket in 1170 and became a significant site of Christian pilgrimage very shortly afterwards. Two centuries later the foibles of at least some pilgrims were described for the delight of posterity by Geoffrey Chaucer.

I stayed at one of the inns along the ancient pilgrim route as recently as last year and was very disappointed in the changes which have taken place since I last visited Canterbury.

However, it was a still the unspoilt city – with all its historic dignity and Christian significance intact – which Michael Powell's and Emeric Pressburger's *A Canterbury Tale* sought to celebrate.

The overriding sensibility of their remarkable film was, in fact, part of a great outpouring of rural romanticism which swept Britain during the years of the Second World War.

Fighting for King and Country became almost indistinguishable for many from battling for King and Countryside – even for those brought up in industrial cities. A bucolic pantheism elided seamlessly with a kind of secularised Christianity.

Indeed, secularised Christianity once provided much of the necessary social cement in most Western countries including Australia but this has by now become replaced increasingly by uneasy agglomerations of fashionable post-modernist orthodoxies and little else. Thus a typical Australian may 'believe' today only in political correctness and climate change, say, and may even consider Christianity as well as all other major world religions to be as outmoded and ridiculous as the wearing of flared trousers.

For the reasons suggested above, the entire world view expressed in *A Canterbury Tale* may now seem incomprehensible to many although the film was first screened only 65 years ago. Yet the same kind of incomprehension would certainly not greet cinematic social comedies of the 1930s nor action-packed war films from a decade or more later.

The underlying theme of *A Canterbury Tale* was different especially because although it dealt with physical realities such as the devastation caused to large areas of that city by German bombing – damage I personally remember clearly from my childhood – its real motif was metaphysical: that all of our actions will be judged ultimately by some higher authority even than that of the highest courts of our land.

In an essay written about the film in 1987 Nannette Aldred remarked: "In times of political crises, British culture tends to turn to its rural roots as a motif of continuity and so did Powell and Pressburger in *A Canterbury Tale*."

The four main characters of the film are a somewhat mysterious and, at times, sinister rural land-owner, a bright female shop-assistant turned wartime 'land-girl', an American GI and an organ-playing British soldier. Their stories and lives interweave against historic backdrops: thus the GI spends a night when on leave in a four-poster bed once slept in by Queen Elizabeth I.

The film enjoyed government support, funding and distribution and was thus to some extent, at least, an instrument of attempted propaganda – especially in its presentation of a view of England to American servicemen many of whom were destined to die in the forthcoming attempt to liberate Western Europe.

Yet *A Canterbury Tale* amounted to something much more than mere propaganda, being brilliantly shot, lit, scripted, directed and – on the whole – acted. Its musical score and choice of unforgettable locations were generally imaginative and at times superb.

A Canterbury Tale remains relevant today not simply because of what it tells us about an era only some of us may still remember but also, by reflection, about the kind of society we have ourselves become.

Can you imagine an Australian war propaganda film being made today in which a cathedral – let alone Christianity – play central, starring roles?

If you can then possibly we have largely become hypocrites who find a use for God only when *in extremis*.

Canterbury cathedral, the building of which was begun in the 12th century, was merely one of 600 magnificent cathedrals and great churches which were constructed across Europe in the heyday of Gothic building to standards of design and construction we can only marvel at today.

What are we to make of such extraordinary structures in our present age?

Are they merely relics of a lost and complex civilisation we can no longer even begin to comprehend?

Like most other local children of my day many of my childhood memories concern war – an interesting cross-section of which, in aerial form at least, took place in the skies above the garden of my family's house.

Eventually such memories fade – until re-awakened suddenly and unexpectedly perhaps by a truly remarkable film.

Children of my day, especially boys, generally prided themselves on the highly useful skill – in terms of self-preservation at least – of 'aircraft recognition'. Indeed, the sole mistake I remember making myself was waving enthusiastically at a squadron of German fighter-bombers as they flew very low in the sky across our garden. These were not, in fact, the new Royal Airforce Typhoons as I had wrongly imagined them to be but Focke-Wulf 190s on their way to bomb and strafe the streets of Canterbury in rumoured retaliation for the bombing by the RAF – whether accidental or otherwise – of Cologne cathedral.

By odd coincidence the day of the attack coincided with the opening of the hugely popular film *Gone with the Wind* in that city which was attended by my mother. A very long queue had in fact formed in the streets outside the cinema which was not far itself from Canterbury Cathedral.

As the low-flying German aircraft opened fire all those in the queue, including my mother, hurled themselves promptly to the ground.

Indeed, what angered my mother much more even than the attack itself was the sight of the lone upright figure of a man who was calmly walking among the prone mainly female figures and helping himself happily to their handbags.

War does indeed throw up some fairly odd situations and we were thus extremely relieved when my irate but film-loving mother finally returned safely to our home.

The Australian 2009, commissioned but unpublished

29

HOME OR AWAY: A WRITER'S DILEMMA

For the first time in years the ABC's recent two-part television panegyric *Brilliant Creatures: Germaine, Clive, Barry and Bob* prompted me to consider the role of the expatriate writer – perhaps because I seem to be one of those myself.

I am sure you will be able to fill in the missing surnames of the famous Australian quartet listed above all of whom made the major part of their considerable reputations through working overseas.

Yet perhaps I might be forgiven here – if only on the basis of my own experience – for wondering what might have happened to any or all of them if they had been obliged, for some strange reason, to remain in Australia.

Might not the rumoured parochialism of Australian life – including that even of famous national institutions such as the ABC – slowly have stifled and finally have submerged their unusual talents?

Ironically, of course, it was the provincialism of Australian life itself which formed a major part of the subject matter which propelled two of the famous four – Clive James and Barry Humphries – to international fame.

Barry Humphries may indeed be one of the few genuine artistic geniuses to have emerged from Australia in the past half century of so.

I was reminded especially of the extreme acuity of his ear and eye some years ago when standing in a long queue at one of the cafeterias at Sydney airport while the cause of the lengthy tailback –

an Australian matron clad in a clinging trouser suit of somewhat vivid hue – explained the virtues of Vegemite at length to a bewildered-looking Asian girl at the cash register.

Even the real Dame Edna might have found it hard to compete.

I wonder here also what might have happened to the late Robert Hughes – who once seemed almost worshipped in this country – if he had been compelled to write his witty and perceptive columns about art here rather than in America?

Might he have been told by a prominent arts editor here – as I have been – that the whole basis of his critical judgement was of little value if it failed to be based on 'Marxist analysis'? Thankfully I do not think 'Marxist analysis' was around in the days when Robert and I first forged our critical careers. Both of us began as painters, in fact, which provided us with a different, but very valuable form of critical insight.

What writers from overseas can evidently bring to their host countries – providing these latter are willing to accommodate them – is a fresh and entirely different approach.

Australia, in my view, has consistently underperformed in all of the arts due largely but not entirely to our continent's physical isolation.

Thus I was in Britain nearly a year ago when our massive, home-produced would-be blockbuster AUSTRALIA was voted by many discerning people there to be the worst major British art exhibition of the year.

But as I wrote in *Annals* at the time such failure was entirely unnecessary for the show was not lacking either in goodwill, a great deal of honest effort or proper financial backing.

What it lacked entirely however was an appreciation of the standards modern international audiences currently expect. As an Australian citizen of fairly recent vintage I felt especially sorry and frustrated by this whole affair.

At first sight Australia appears to be a typically modern, prosperous Western country but the reality can often be quite different. Frequently, in fact, Australia fiercely resists precisely the kind of international input this country needs most.

This last applies particularly perhaps to Australian academic as well as to Australian artistic life.

In the case of the former modish post-modernist individuals and ideas are often still clutched to the national academic bosom here long after their international use-by dates have expired.

For example, when I first came to Australia to work fashionable, French quasi-philosophers Jacques Derrida and Michel Foucault could apparently say or do no wrong here even though the reputations and ideas of both had already been effectively demolished by the English philosopher Roger Scruton in Derrida's case and the American Roger Kimball in that of Foucault.

Both Scruton and Kimball have recently conducted successful lecture tours in Australia.

Kimball personally sent me a copy of his excellent anthology *Experiments against Reality* (Ivan R.Dee Chicago 2000) when it was first published. This was the book in which his excellent critical essay on Foucault first appeared.

When Jacques Derrida lectured at Sydney Town Hall in the early 2000s all available seats had been block-booked by the University of Sydney and I cannot help wondering now whether any similar enthusiasm was shown by such institutions for the recent talks given locally by Scruton and Kimball even though both are respected international figures.

Indeed, if any such enthusiasm were not shown what would you expect the reason to be?

The short answer is that both of these writers are filed by Australia's academic Left in pigeon-holes marked Christian and conservative. Indeed, which of the latter epithets is more unacceptable here in current left-wing academic circles would be hard to say.

If you consult *The Oxford Companion to Australian History*, a large volume which purports to be our definitive national handbook you will find that communism is treated more sympathetically than conservatism in the course of long articles devoted to both subjects.

Might that be because two of the three editors of that 'invaluable' research document are or were communists themselves?

When then did my own personal experience of Australia begin and start to take shape?

During the 11 years in which I wrote weekly articles in England for *The Spectator* I filed copy from some twenty foreign countries which included such slightly fraught communist or ex-communist destinations of the day as Georgia, Slovenia and the former USSR itself.

Thus what could I possibly have to fear by accepting an overseas post in Australia where I at least shared a common language?

In the event a chorus of violent disapproval greeted my arrival here in 1995 in which *The Age* and 'our' ABC played prominent roles. *The Age* ran a very hostile half-page composed entirely from interviews with left-wing UK journalists known to disagree with my views while, by contrast, the ABC concocted a lengthy and extremely dishonestly edited TV feature made up largely from hostile comments by Australians I had yet to meet.

To cap it all perhaps a prominent ABC radio interviewer explained to someone I knew exactly why she declined to talk to me: "I can't possibly have people *like that* on my show".

At times I felt tempted to wonder whether my plane from London had perhaps landed in North Korea by mistake.

Was the aim to prove to me that any suspected of traditionally-based views on art – or any other subject – are most unwelcome here?

It was at that juncture that I received an amiable call from a man often characterised as being a traditionalist or conservative himself: a former Catholic Archbishop of Melbourne.

The purpose of his call was to enlist my advice regarding possible improvements to St.Patrick's Cathedral. These included a proposed 3 metre bronze of a famous predecessor there: Archbishop Mannix.

The good Archbishop had been reading my articles for years in *The Spectator* and, from what he knew, was confident to place the latter project entirely in my hands. This was perhaps fortunate for both of us because commissioning specialist works of art was an area in which I had some lengthy and useful experience.

While working on this particular project I also had the great pleasure of meeting the late B.A.Santamaria. Previously we had known each other only through our published writings.

Several months later when the day of the official unveiling of the bronze created by English sculptor Nigel Boonham finally arrived, I asked not to sit with the official party so that I would be free to gauge the reactions of the gathered crowd.

"Tis the man" an elderly man of Irish extraction – who had probably known Archbishop Mannix quite well – shouted at the precise moment of the unveiling.

In my view no greater compliment could have been paid to the sculptor's extremely diligent research and months of hard and skilful work.

Before the actual moment of the unveiling the last I had seen of the sculpture myself was when it was no more than two tons of moulded clay on an armature. My wife and I even helped to sheet the clay up to prevent it drying out. This took place at the sculptor's studio in London.

It was a great pleasure to encounter this fine work once more in its final imposing form.

> • I especially salute the recent elevation of the former Catholic Archbishop of Melbourne – known better today as Cardinal Pell – to a vital role at the Vatican because he was much criticised in Australia for his unwavering support for the essential doctrines and traditions of the Catholic Church.
>
> • In passing, perhaps we should all reflect here that if all the so-called 'progressives' in the history of the Catholic Church had had their way, the Church would by now be totally unrecognisable – and greatly diminished in its purpose here on earth.
>
> • As such, in fact, it would simply echo the historic fates

which have befallen most of the major art forms of the
civilised world.

Annals, October 2014

30

STRANGE COINCIDENCE OR SOMETHING ELSE?

Towards the end of his life my late and sorely missed friend Frank Devine, a former editor of *The Australian*, wrote some 67 essays for the excellent Australian literary monthly *Quadrant*.

Following Frank's death in 2009 the publishing arm of that magazine republished just over half of these entertaining and thoughtful pieces in the form of a book appropriately named *Older & Wiser*.

Unfortunately for all of us the reality of growing older – unlike various forms of self-induced misfortune – remains non-negotiable in spite of the strenuous efforts some of us may make to keep physical decrepitude at bay.

Unlike my former colleague Frank I did not begin my professional life as a journalist but first endeavoured instead – after a number of false starts – to forge some kind of career as a professional painter.

During a period of two decades – roughly from 1960 to 1980 – I spent well over half of my time living in West Cornwall at the extreme South Westerly tip of Britain in days when that small area of ancient land with its glorious surrounding seas probably contained more truly excellent painters, potters, sculptors, poets and other writers – who together comprised the local, so-called artists' colony – than we will probably ever see grouped together in any rural area again.

I was very lucky indeed, in short, to have lived a significant part of my early life among people to whom the creative arts and crafts were absolutely fundamental to their daily existence.

Jealousies and fallings-out did certainly occur yet mutual belief in the vital human importance of maintaining a vibrant culture never seemed in serious doubt even for a moment.

At the end of days of concentrated painting I usually turned my attention instead to a desk and typewriter which were situated handily close to my studio's large main window. Much as I loved painting I experienced an increasing but unexplained urge at about that time also to write about the subject of art not least because I felt that so many others were making rather a poor job of explaining art's perennial issues to their reading publics. In the meantime, both my painting and writing were probably aided by looking out from the studio window onto Mount's Bay, one of the more beautiful marine vistas in the world.

My parallel life as a writer and future journalist thus properly began not in the fashionable hurly-burly of a newspaper office but in a state of almost total isolation and of a silence broken only by the occasional cries of gulls which were passing my window.

In the eyes of many journalists, I suspect, what I have just written may well disqualify me permanently from being considered as any kind of 'proper' writer at all.

Although I exhibited my paintings regularly at a private art gallery in London the usual consequence even of a successful exhibition – at the prices I was then able to command – seldom achieved anything much more than a temporary paying off of my habitual bank overdraft.

The beginning of the 1980s therefore found me very relieved indeed to accept a teaching post at an art school near London – a stint of four years which unfortunately ended with a final phasing out there of the Fine Arts course.

What on earth to do next?

One evening just before the final ending of the course I was unusually late in arriving at the local railway station to catch my train home.

As a result I had to sprint to catch the train at all and thus had no time to buy my usual evening paper. However fellow commuters often discarded their copies of that paper by simply leaving them behind them on the train.

Having just managed to board the very last carriage as the train began moving, I then walked the entire length of a largely empty train before finally finding the paper I sought.

Happily the copy that I found of that particular afternoon's *Evening Standard* was also folded so strangely that a tiny article on an inner page – which I could very easily have missed – was brought unavoidably to my attention.

The headline simply read ART CRITIC RESIGNS.

Reading on from there I learned that the resignation had happened at the respected British magazine *The Spectator* where their well-known critic had resigned as a sign of his disapproval at the sacking of the journal's then editor, Alexander Chancellor.

Some years earlier the book about art I had written 'after hours' in my painting studio had been reviewed very favourably by that paper.

More in hope than expectation I telephoned the only person I then knew at *The Spectator* as soon as I arrived home.

At least partly as a result of that basic happy if extremely unlikely chance I shortly found myself appointed – after a relatively brief period of trial – as that paper's new art critic. Thus began the very happy journalistic career into which I had first stumbled almost entirely by accident.

In the latter part of his professional life my late father helped revise major international dictionaries – including the Complete Oxford English Dictionary – for a living while my sole sibling worked, by contrast, as a researcher for some years for one of the world's better-known encyclopaedias.

I must confess that such dry-seeming academic exercises never held any great appeal for me. Indeed, in marked contrast to my better-organised father and sister I arrived at my own latter choice of career seemingly by complete chance.

While most intelligent people have a good grasp of the meaning of the word vocation in relation to members of religious orders how many people recall today that such lay professions as medicine and nursing were once also widely considered to be 'callings'?

What then precisely is a 'calling' and what is simply a career?

In our increasingly irreligious times it may also be appropriate to ask who it is precisely who is doing any 'calling'?

Indeed, how many people in the general community will even bother their heads with such a curious-seeming question today?

In my eleven very happy years with *The Spectator* I visited roughly 500 exhibitions a year, in a variety of countries, and ended up writing more or less exactly that number of articles for the magazine itself.

Can art criticism ever be described truly as a vocation?

In my case at least, destiny – whatever we may agree destiny to be – once certainly seemed to lend me rather an obvious and very welcome helping hand.

When I came to Australia twenty years ago I continued to write criticism for a further seven years and since then have been very lucky in the encouragement I have received to write regularly about other subjects generally unconnected to the arts.

However unobvious this may seem I believe the discipline of writing intelligible criticism about the complexities of art – whether ancient or modern – provides a very useful aid in unravelling many of the complexities of modern living themselves.

Possibly the first thing all writers need to learn, in fact, is that before one can explain any complex matter clearly to anyone else it is first necessary to explain it at least as clearly to oneself.

However, when I began writing criticism forty years ago most practitioners preferred instead to write prose of such impenetrable density as to defy even the most earnest attempts at understanding.

What possible purposes did such writing serve?

When I started out on my own tardy and largely unplanned critical career I therefore resolved that I would not write even a single sentence which failed in the intention to be understood.

Over the years I seem to have written roughly a million words of published criticism – quite apart from other, unrelated writings – and challenge readers to find even a single sentence they are unable to understand – unless a misprint has somehow slipped in.

During the coming year, following the example of the late Frank Devine, I hope to publish at least some of my collected essays in book form covering quite a wide range of subjects. If I am successful this should give at least a few more potential readers the time and leisure to accept my challenge.

While making sense is one thing, the question of the opinion expressed is clearly another matter entirely.

Today I am regularly astonished by the number of persons and authorities who express vehement opinions which seem to bear no relationship whatsoever to their areas of supposed expertise.

Indeed, simply in the past few days I have thus learned that ANZ Bank 'proudly' co-sponsored Sydney's recent Gay and Lesbian Mardi Gras – which one must surely take as an expression of pretty strong support – and that Blue Mountains City Council, to whom I would prefer simply to pay my rates, currently supports Gay Marriage on the apparent grounds of its superior 'fairness'.

Are not certain people somewhat exceeding their areas of agreed authority by expressing such views?

Is it also purely a matter simply of coincidence that such areas of apparent bias are almost always hostile to traditional Christian teaching?

I was also mildly surprised to read an art review in a major Australian newspaper recently which launched off with what seemed like a sentiment of profound religious scepticism:

> The religious life of most people is a composite of overlaid and interwoven traditions, sometimes quite disparate in origin; this is true notwithstanding the common tendency of humans to persuade themselves that their own particular system is a special, superior and definitive dispensation expressly granted them by a supernatural mandate long ago, far away and in circumstances conveniently free of witnesses".

One cannot help wondering now which other major Australian bank will be the first 'proudly' to sponsor euthanasia for example?

In the meantime may I express a profound hope that my dry cleaners will not be sponsoring anything soon other than the excellent cleaning service which they provide so regularly for my clothes?

Annals, March 2015

31

BLUE POLES & THE NOVELTY TRAP

A FEW MONTHS BACK, a rash of articles appeared in the press which commemorated the dismissal of the Whitlam government thirty years ago and commented on the continuing sense of grievance felt by his supporters. At the time, I wondered how much more could usefully be written on the subject.

By contrast, an event of almost equal notoriety if not importance had taken place in Australia some two years before the dismissal which has never been explored or explained satisfactorily. I refer to the purchase of Jackson Pollock's *Blue Poles* in August 1973 by what was then called the Australian National Gallery.

In the ten years that I have lived in Australia so far, I have often heard the view expressed – in leftist circles especially – that the buying of *Blue Poles* provided a catalyst for Australia's cultural coming-of-age. According to this received wisdom an increasingly confident nation – inspired by the leadership of Gough Whitlam – not only bought itself a wonderful work of art but an outstanding bargain at the same time.

Many might feel disappointed if neither of these facts proved true. Indeed, until the significance or otherwise of the painting itself and the circumstances surrounding its purchase are dragged belatedly into sharper focus, *Blue Poles* may yet prove to have been a hindrance to the attainment of national cultural maturity rather than the reverse.

Perhaps the first part of the myth to dispel is that Australia plucked an outstanding bargain from under the noses of older and more established museums overseas. What Australia really seems to have done is buy itself a monument to a formerly fashionable but highly questionable notion of artistic progress. Indeed, no sooner had the painting arrived here than this notion found itself the subject of increasingly vocal international critical attack.

To put it another way, *Blue Poles* could be said to represent a kind of last hurrah for an outdated and weirdly monolinear conception of the evolution of art. Indeed, by the time Pollock had painted it, he and his friends were openly declaring that painting had "nowhere left to go" and could be followed henceforward only by "performance" art.

I will return to this issue of evolution a little later. For the present, I should begin perhaps with a subject which seems to grab public attention much more readily than the vested and supposedly insoluble issue of artistic merit. In short, how much exactly is the damned thing worth?

Current guesses – and that is all any of them are – about the current market value of Blue Poles range from US$20 million to a highly improbable US$100 million but the accuracy or otherwise of these guesses cannot, of course, ever be tested unless the work is offered for sale. At the time of its purchase in 1973, the price paid – US$2 million – represented only A$1.3 million.

So if we take US$20 million as a realistic starting point for the current market value of *Blue Poles*, it becomes apparent that it has increased in value by at least ten times during the thirty-three years Australia has owned it. However, this by no means represents the greatest recorded acceleration in its market value. In 1953, three years before Jackson Pollock's untimely demise, the American dealer Sidney Janis sold *Blue Poles* to Dr Fred Olson for $6000. But shortly after Pollock managed to kill himself and one other by driving when unfit to do so, Ben Heller – another American dealer – was prepared to pay $32,000 for the work.

In art, nothing can compare with death as a means of jacking up market prices. But if we take 1953 as our starting point, the next twenty years, culminating with the purchase of *Blue Poles* for the Australian nation, saw its price rise by a giddy 166 times. Even in the sixteen years after Heller bought it its market price rose thirty times. In other words, the last thirty-three years have witnessed a sharp slowing down of the rate of increase of its supposed market worth.

I am tempted to suggest that if the Australian National Gallery had forked out US$2 million in 1973 on purchasing housing in the Canberra area – in preference to *Blue Poles* – the gross return on its investment might well have been greater. Yet the notion that Australia made a uniquely inspired purchase in monetary terms is only part of a greater myth which continues to surround Blue Poles. Surely no less to the point is whether *Blue Poles* really is an outstanding work of art.

WHERE MIGHT WE TURN for informed opinions? What about starting with the artist himself? In Florence Rubenfeld's biography of the American art critic Clement Greenberg (*Clement Greenberg: A Life*, 1997) we have Greenberg's word that Pollock himself considered *Blue Poles* "a failure". But Greenberg, who was probably Pollock's most consistent supporter, was even more dismissive, declaring unequivocally that *Blue Poles* was "an absolute failure and a ridiculous thing to buy". This comment is reported in Patricia Anderson's biography of the late Elwyn Lynn, *Elwyn Lynn's Art World* (2001). Lynn was my predecessor as art critic for *The Australian*.

But *Blue Poles* did not lack professional supporters at the time of its purchase. Indeed yet another former art critic for the Australian, whose tenure there (1972–84) comfortably exceeded my own, certainly did not share any of Pollock's or Greenberg's misgivings about *Blue Poles*. Writing in the *Weekend Australian* of August 25, 1973, Sandra McGrath evidently preferred the enthusiasm shown by New York-based Australian art dealer Max Hutchinson – who personally brokered the sale of Blue Poles to the Australian National Gallery – to the reservations expressed by Pollock himself and Greenberg.

Dipping deep into her handbag of superlatives, McGrath proclaimed that "the purchase of *Blue Poles* is the most momentous event in the cultural history of Australia" and "Jackson

Pollock is … the artist whose work made it impossible for painting ever to look quite the same again". Max Hutchinson proposed that "*Blue Poles*, along with Picasso's *Guernica* and Monet's *Waterlilies*, is one of the five or six great works of art painted since the Renaissance". Perhaps embarrassed by the enormity of her colleague's claim, McGrath nevertheless chipped in with "it is certainly one of the five or six great paintings of the twentieth century".

These are certainly extravagant claims which cannot begin to be taken seriously unless both Hutchinson and McGrath were known to have an unusually encyclopaedic grasp of art history. This would certainly be unusual in the case of a dealer. If I had been working here at the time, I would have been keen indeed to ask Mr Hutchinson which particular artists he would have picked to fill his last two or three available slots as producers of "the five or six great works of art painted since the Renaissance".

The task of choosing between the lifetime productions of the likes of Caravaggio, Velazquez, Rembrandt, Vermeer, Veronese, Tiepolo, Goya, van Gogh, Cezanne, Manet, Matisse and Picasso – to name just a handy dozen – would certainly be a daunting one even for someone thoroughly familiar with the greatest works of all twelve.

An altogether more sensible question might be whether *Blue Poles* could be said to rank even in the top five or six of Pollock's own productions. On the basis of the definitive exhibition of Pollock's art I saw when it was staged by the Tate Gallery in London in 1999, I would argue that it could not. I imagine that a number of other professional commentators who are similarly familiar with Pollock's work would agree with me.

Yet evidently most of those who gawp daily at *Blue Poles* on the walls of what is now called the National Gallery of Australia cannot be expected to share this degree of familiarity with Pollock's work. Indeed, few members of the public who have seen *Blue Poles* at that venue will ever come face to face with any other work by Pollock. Unavoidably, therefore, most members of the public will be largely reliant on hearsay and the fact that the work is seemingly legitimised by where it hangs in forming any conclusion at all about its merits.

In the event, the fact that anything hangs on the walls of the National Gallery of Australia or on those of the principal galleries of Australia's states should not be looked on as any guarantee of anything, since all have proved pretty fallible at times in their buying policies.

As recently as 1999, for instance, the National Gallery of Australia made a colossal error of judgment not just by buying David Hockney's huge (744 centimetre) and weakly conceived *A Bigger Grand Canyon* but by paying a grossly inflated price for it (over A$4 million). No less to the point, that same institution only months earlier had turned down the chance to acquire a truly magnificent giant landscape (810 centimetre) by a homebred artist. This was William Robinson's *Creation Series: The Ancient Trees*, which also carried a rather more realistic price tag of A$250,000.

What I am suggesting with regret is that the standards of judgment shown by Australia's national and principal state galleries are frequently inept. Generally this is because judgment is skewed by predilections for fashion and temporary fame and because curators and directors have managed to persuade themselves somehow that novelty must be a virtue in itself.

The reason why the latter trait has become so firmly entrenched deserves urgent investigation. My own explanation centres on the insidious role played by what I call "the rhetoric of radicalism" in creating current and recent artistic climates.

RHETORIC, AS WE KNOW, describes language designed to persuade or impress. Its natural habitat is politics and advertising but, in both of those fields, long acquaintance has led intelligent minds to recognise its nature and dilute its effectiveness. Regrettably, the full toxicity of such language still takes effect in areas where the ubiquity of its use remains unrecognised. In no area is this truer than in the visual arts.

The twentieth century, which was dominated by modernism in the visual arts, saw the rise and fall of about forty readily identifiable and supposedly significant art movements in the Western world alone.

Can there really have been an art movement for every two and a half years of an entire century? No other hundred-year period can even begin to compare with the twentieth century in this regard. And who today, other than specialist art historians, can give an accurate account of what Orphism, say, or Rayonism were? Yet in their heydays many people believed wholeheartedly in the significance of both movements.

So what was it precisely that first led to the obsession with novelty in art which has never gone away?

Though few seem to have made a serious effort to define what does or does not constitute modernism in any of the arts, its most evident and unifying characteristic clearly has to be rejection of past ideas and practices. Indeed, if such rejection is absent we are not really talking about modernism at all. For a modernist label to apply, the break with past practice has to be total.

Thus when, at the conclusion of the First World War, Picasso – whom many might consider the epitome of the modern artist – embarked on a series of neo-classical works as an oblique tribute to Renoir, his erstwhile collaborator in Cubism, Georges Braque, was quick to accuse him of "betraying modernism".

From the outset, modernism in art, which liked to portray itself as a liberating force, had its own rigid set of prohibitions. In short, modernism's paid-up followers were free to do anything they chose *with the exception of maintaining any overt links with a pre-modern past.*

Two linked factors underlay the seemingly inexorable elevation of formal radicalism in art to a position of effective dominance. The more obvious of the two was the conscious or subconscious but ultimately unjustified connection many people made naively between the evident and very real advances which were taking place in other, unrelated disciplines – in medicine, say, or powered flight – with what was happening in art roughly at the same time. Yet the less obvious of the two factors was certainly no less influential. This was the way radical practices in the arts – taking their cue from technology – first attracted to themselves and then virtually annexed a wholly favourable rhetorical language.

In short, to situate oneself on the side of what many claimed was "inevitable" progress – or advance, development, evolution, breakthrough or "fearless" experimentation – was to place oneself, rhetorically at least, fairly and squarely in the camp of the angels. By seizing for its own purposes the positive, propagandist language associated with claimed progress in other fields, modernism in art ensured for itself for the foreseeable future a very unlevel playing field wherein even the most acute and perceptive criticism could be dismissed airily as conservative, reactionary or – worst of all perhaps – as being "opposed to progress".

Carried away by its borrowed rhetoric, the elementary truth that modernism chose to ignore here is that there are two equally vital traditions and sources of influence in art – *as well as in all other aspects of human behaviour* – the radical and the continuous. Perhaps the most damaging legacy of modernism has thus been the part radicalist rhetoric has played in obscuring so obvious a truth from so many for so long. To cite merely one obvious example, it would be impossible to be wholly modernistic or radical in one's ideas and at the same time be a committed Christian. Christianity antedates modernism by a little matter of 1900 years and thus is part of a continuous tradition.

Perhaps the most apt parallel one might find for modernism is Marxism, since both, in a sense, attempted to rewrite history by subverting and stamping out existing ideas and practices. Although both ideologies had their roots in nineteenth-century thinking, neither came to full flower before the first and second decades of the twentieth century. Both also held out explicit or implicit promises of the future triumphs which would attend their causes: the final victory of the proletariat and a kind of artistic apotheosis which would mark the culmination of the oddly one-track model of artistic evolution which modernists favoured.

There is little doubt that it was this kind of crowning achievement which the modernist faithful believed they discerned in the subconsciously-driven "action" paintings of Jackson Pollock. It is this apotheosis, rather than a fairly incoherent mass of paint which attempts to redeem itself through the use of unusual vertical bars, which all of us are supposed to see when gazing at *Blue Poles*.

Yet I doubt whether even one in a hundred visitors to the National Gallery of Australia has the least inkling of this. Indeed, I am reminded of a comment made when Blue Poles was first revealed to an expectant Australian public: "I had rather hoped it would be bluer."

When Australia managed to "beat down" Ben Heller in 1973 from an asking price of US $3 million to a "bargain" price of $2 million, both figures were plucked strictly from fantasy-land. As expatriate Australian art critic Robert Hughes remarked somewhat sourly when delivering the Harold Rosenberg Lecture at the University of Chicago in 1984:

> My fellow countrymen were rather proud of beating Ben Heller's creative asking price down from $3 million. Nobody had even thought of asking so much for a Pollock; but of course the market gratefully rallied behind this heroic example and every Pollock in the world quintupled in price overnight, thus enabling the National Gallery of Australia to announce that *Blue Poles* was really cheap…

Clearly the National Gallery of Australia has a vested interest in maintaining its selfcreated myth of prescience and inspired financial acumen in the matter of *Blue Poles*. But surely the time has come now to put the merits or otherwise of the painting itself into some more credible perspective.

WHAT IS BASICALLY WRONG with the Pollock is also what is wrong with the arguments for modernism themselves: to wit, to suggest that the narrative of Western art should be read as a kind of art-historical relay race which culminates in the death of painting simply because there are no more apparent avenues of novelty left to explore is both spurious and infantile. If a map of modernism is largely a chart of cul-de-sacs then the time has come to admit this.

Jackson Pollock, despite his long history of alcoholism and failed attempts at remedial therapy, had a much more cogent appreciation of the dangers of artistic dead ends than that shown subsequently by his apologists. *Blue Poles* belongs to a period of his work of which the artist himself had grown weary. In fact, the type of "all-over" abstract painting to which *Blue Poles* broadly belongs occupied only a relatively brief interlude even within the parameters of Pollock's truncated career. Ample evidence exists that if he had lived longer he would have worked very differently. Before and after *Blue Poles* and the short era of other poured and dripped paintings, Pollock's work featured a variety of clearly recognisable imagery drawn – or perhaps wrestled – from his troubled subconscious.

Pollock taught himself to pour and drip paint with a singular, highly developed and

concentrated skill and in so doing successfully sidestepped the relative clumsiness of his more directly manual mark-making. As Robert Hughes remarked in 1982, Pollock "was by no means a natural draftsman and his best paintings of the early forties … are set down with earnestness but no graphic facility".

No one with any knowledge of the subject would deny that there is a validity of a kind in abstract painting and that attempts to resolve wholly abstract works seem to bring into play processes of "pure" intuition which can be extraordinarily exhilarating for the artist involved. At times the artist's hand seems to be a direct conduit for unknown forces; out of the blue, the receptive artist suddenly feels a "need" for a small, bright yellow, triangular shape near the top right hand corner of his canvas…

But the question remains as to whether such a process can genuinely be said to mark the culmination of all the centuries of much more deliberate-seeming and humanistically relevant painting which had gone before. Then, too, there is the matter of the belief that modernists hold that the history of art should be read largely in the light of the supposed contributions earlier artists made to a process which culminated in "total" abstraction. Major artists as various as Whistler and Turner are regularly recruited posthumously – and thus involuntarily – to this cause.

As someone who sees the history of art as seamless, I would argue strenuously against both of these propositions. Let us imagine for a moment that I am stood simultaneously in front of *Blue Poles*, Titian's *The Flaying of Marsyas* (1570–76), *The Surrender of Breda* (1634–35) by Velazquez, and Goya's *Fantastic Vision* (1819–23) – to cite merely three points of comparison from thousands available – could I put my hand on my heart and say I see Pollock's painting as an "advance" on the other three? The simple answer is I could not, and suspect that many others who are familiar with all four works would agree with me.

The big problem here from the point of view of the Australian public is that any such exercise becomes harder to imagine because of the relative inaccessibility of major works by earlier generations of European artists. Two of the four paintings I have cited can normally be seen only in Madrid while a third, by Titian, is more inaccessible still.

It seems to me the whole notion of modernism and modernistic "progress" can survive only in a kind of vacuum where all evidence of the staggering artistic feats of the past is deliberately ignored, or misunderstood, or expunged from memory, or – as is the tragic case of Australia – is largely unavailable for assessment. To believe *Blue Poles* is one of "the five or six great works of art painted since the Renaissance" – as Max Hutchinson averred – can stem only from infantile delusion or utter unfamiliarity with the world's great collections of art.

As I suggested earlier, ignorant idolisation of *Blue Poles* locks Australia into a situation of cultural backwardness which only the conscientious teaching of art history and compulsory visits to the world's great collections of art could even begin to address.

The basic reason why I do not believe *Blue Poles* represents any kind of qualitative advance on the three paintings I chose above, more or less at random, from three earlier centuries, lies beyond anything in its incoherence and self-absorption. I cannot imagine for a moment that Titian, Velazquez and Goya would ever have believed that a day would come when simply dribbling or pouring paint onto a support might be looked on as a worthwhile end in itself.

The very late Titian I have chosen, painted between the artist's eighty-fifth year and his death at ninety-one, is extraordinarily expressive and free yet also brilliantly considered in the way it organises seven figures and a dog in portraying a terrifying subject from pagan mythology. The degree of imagination shown is stupendous, as it is in the relatively early Velazquez I have cited, painted when the artist was just thirty-five.

The huge Velazquez, which chronicles an actual historical event, is no less brilliant in its organisation of multiple figures, landscape and complex sky. The clarity, painterly intelligence and graphic skill shown are similarly staggering. How can an incoherent mass of marks by Pollock, covering roughly the same surface area as the Velazquez, possibly be said to compare with it?

Regress, rather than progress, leaps to mind here, yet the great claim made by Pollock's apologists is that he "went beyond" Velazquez's fellow countrymen Miro and Picasso. But was the direction in which Pollock supposedly "went further" ever remotely worth travelling? In my experience this is just the sort of question which modernists avoid.

From quite an early stage Pollock's art was rooted in the subconscious yet contributes nothing in particular to our knowledge of the subject. Contrast this with the intriguing, metaphysical nature of Goya's *Fantastic Vision*, which features two flying figures – or witches – who are being shot at by earthbound soldiers. One of the flying figures gestures towards a citadel on a hill. Although fantastic, the scene is hauntingly credible, like a miraculously direct delineation of a meaningful dream.

I DO NOT WISH to single out Australia as displaying anything nationally unique in the way of uninformed artistic attitudes. Without intelligent programs of education, confidently pursued, ignorant artistic attitudes are more than likely to be internationally widespread.

As some small evidence of this, the following conversation took place recently in Britain between David Lee, a Courtauld-trained art historian and admirably forthright art critic, and someone who sounds like a youngish if invincibly opinionated artist. The conversation was reported in the July-August 2005 edition of *Jackdaw*, a newsletter for the visual arts edited by Lee:

"During a recent meeting I got a damn good ticking off from an artist. 'Art can't stand still,' she asserted as though rote-repeating a Commandment. 'We have to progress and move on.' 'Move on?' I enquired, baffled. 'Where to?' "She believed it to be an incontrovertible truth that in order for a work of art to be taken seriously it had to 'progress' beyond what had been done before. If it didn't it wasn't worth registering; indeed to repeat what had already happened was in her eyes scarcely less than a crime. "I told her I had no idea what she was talking about and that her conviction that only 'the new' could be important or enjoyable played no part in the way I looked at or interpreted any kind of art past or present."

This conversation epitomises the worrying way in which the basic thoughtlessness of the classic modernist standpoint continues to remain entrenched. In saying that, the sentiments expressed by the young artist could be encountered just as easily at the Australia Council or National Gallery of Australia. I intend no particular disparagement to either body.

As is clear from the confidence of the young artist's attitude, she feels – so far as art goes – that the idea that novelty is automatically a virtue in itself has been legitimised sufficiently to make further debate unnecessary. In pursuit of this notion, it may be instructive to look at the kind of means which first seemed to legitimise and thus institutionalise such an idea.

I quote from Herbert Read, who later received a knighthood and was a highly influential figure in promoting the basic precepts of modernism not only in Britain but internationally. The words are taken from Read's *A Concise History of Modern Painting* (1959), a book which for decades was not merely a standard textbook but also something of a bible on art history courses. The author explains why he has excluded various highly respected artists from his book:

For a similar reason I have excluded realistic painting, by which I
mean the style of painting that continues with little variation the
academic traditions of the nineteenth century. I do not deny the
great accomplishment and permanent value of the work of such
painters as Edward Hopper, Balthus, Christian Berard, or Stanley
Spencer (to make a random list); they certainly belong to the
history of art in our time. But not to the style of painting that is
specifically 'modern'.

The crucial point to note here is that, of the two legitimate
and commonly encountered meanings given to the word *modern*,
Read chose style and attitude rather than period as the basis for his
exclusions. Thus artists who are clearly – and unavoidably – modern
in other respects such as Hopper and Balthus are excluded solely on
the grounds of style, thus effectively making formal radicalism the
most important index of quality whether for inclusion in Read's own
book, a 'modern' collection or a 'modern' museum.

Read, of course, was not solely to blame for what has subsequently
happened. Yet, as a direct consequence of attitudes like Read's, there is
not a single painting by Edward Hopper in a British public collection
and only one damaged example by Balthus. In short, we see how easily
one of the two great traditions in art – the continuous – was effectively
marginalised and banished. By contrast to the treatment of Hopper
and Balthus – two of the great figurative artists of the twentieth
century – by British public galleries, even the most inconsequential
and third-rate artists from overseas have been collected avidly and in
depth for British public collections provided only that they met with
Read's canon of style.

A further, contributing factor to a profoundly unsatisfactory
state of affairs is that it has been widely believed by the unthinking
that endless formal novelty was inexorably dragging art onward and
upward to some unspecified apotheosis. Indeed, that is what the
"rhetoric of radicalism" has been consistently promising all of us but
which has, of course, never been fulfilled.

The meaning we attach to the word *modern* is vital to the future of art; in short, contrary to what modernists believe, novelty of style and attitude is not and never can be a virtue in itself in art or in any other area of life, since all change can always just as easily be for the worse as for the better.

Such a point ought to be self-evident philosophically and – if you are tempted to doubt me – ask yourself whether you believe that radical moral behaviour is automatically superior to established moral codes.

SADLY FOR THE HEALTH of our culture, the fallacy inherent in what I describe as the "novelty trap" has been welcomed and endorsed by almost any cultural body you can think of and most notably, of course, by our Western "modern" museum culture itself.

What is wrong with such culture boils down, as I have suggested already, to a harmfully erroneous idea of what *modern* ought to be held to mean in relation to the arts. In fact, the meaning we attach to the word needs to be entirely neutral – that is, favouring neither radicalism nor continuity in art over each other. In order for this to happen, the meaning we give to the word *modern* in such a context *has to relate solely to period and nothing else.*

I sense that such a fundamental change of emphasis would be favoured not only by most interested members of the public but also by a majority of working artists of all kinds. In short, it is in the interests of only a small – if extremely vocal – minority to try to sell novelty in any of the arts as an automatic virtue.

Imagine for a moment what might have happened if all the publicly funded art galleries

in the world which have collected the art of the past 100 years had been obliged by their charters to deal even-handedly in their collecting policies between art which reflected the best of the continuous as well as radical traditions. One certain result would be that the art on view would be much more varied and interesting – as well as less inaccessible and irritating, on the whole – to those who are obliged, whether they like it or not, to fund such institutions through their taxes. I am not advocating anything which could be described as a greater degree of populism here. Proper standards of achievement should be demanded of those who work in more traditional and continuous ways just as they should be – but frequently are not – of those who flirt consciously and often for advantage with the latest fashions.

The storerooms of Australia's state and national galleries are full to overflowing already with embarrassingly ephemeral art "bought in haste and repented at leisure" by curators, committees and directors who have convinced themselves that novelty must be a virtue somehow, especially where works lack any other obvious merits. Another instant and highly beneficial effect of my suggested change of emphasis would be on art education. Artists desperate to learn time-honoured skills would no longer need to feel disadvantaged academically – as they certainly do now – or in terms of their subsequent careers by not being at the "cutting edge". Indeed, as an absolutely typical example of the tiresomely familiar "rhetoric of radicalism", expressions such as "cutting edge" are overdue for permanent banishment – along with the entire delusion in art of modernistic "progress" itself.

In relation to *Blue Poles*, imagine the relief of many who might no longer feel any obligation to see in it qualities which were never there, but to view it rather as an interesting example of a formerly fashionable way of regarding the evolution of art, once promoted vigorously by an American cultural establishment desperate to create credibility for itself.

To those fortunate enough to be familiar with the greater history of art, both *Blue Poles* itself and the whole, aberrant notion of "total" abstraction in art will continue to appear as very small blips on a very large screen. For the rest, a serious attempt to get the history of art into some kind of focus represents an ideal starting point for showing genuine concern for the future of art in this, or any other country.

Quadrant, April 2006

THE MEANING OF MODERN REVISITED

In what seem now like the rather distant days of 1994 I was invited to give the annual Jack Manton Memorial Lecture at the Art Gallery of New South Wales in Sydney on a subject of my choice. Neil MacGregor, then head of Britain's National Gallery had given the talk there the previous year.

The title of my talk was *The Meaning of Modern* and I have often wondered since then how many of my Australian audience really grasped the rather unlikely-seeming significance of the main point I was trying to make.

While it could be argued quite reasonably that it was largely my fault if they failed to do so there also has to be a degree of receptivity on the part of an audience towards novel or controversial ideas – perhaps especially towards those which defy long-established orthodoxies.

Nonetheless my talk was well attended and was possibly even one of the factors that persuaded the then editor-in-chief of *The Australian* to offer me a job. That was to be the role of national art correspondent covering the whole of Australia.

Regrettably for me the extraordinary majesty and variety of Australia's physical landscape is not always matched by the quality or variety of this country's cultural and intellectual life.

A number of changes of residence later I have long lost touch with the whereabouts of the notes I made all those years ago for my talk – which has also not subsequently been put before any other audience.

I therefore welcomed the chance suggested to me a while ago to run the main theme of the talk, at least, past the discerning readers of the extremely lively British art magazine *The Jackdaw* which, along with *Quadrant, The Spectator* and *Annals,* has provided me with a most welcome lifeline to stimulating intellectual notions during my years of residence in Australia.

The Meaning of Modern

At times the answers to all sorts of matters which regularly perplex us can stare us in the face for a long time before we finally recognise them for what they are.

For me the precise meaning we assign to the word modern falls very much into that category – as I will do my best to explain.

Indeed I suggest here that the whole notion of modernism in any of the arts was seriously flawed from the outset for the good reason that its keenest supporters and promoters became so carried away with what they fondly imagined to be the 'inevitable progress' of art that they failed to foresee the dangers of creating a monster whose greed simply for novelty might ultimately become impossible to sustain

Because of the privileges I formerly enjoyed of being a recognised art critic I have had regular access to the storerooms of a number of national and regional galleries which, over the years, became repositories for a great deal of exceedingly poor and evanescent art which was nevertheless collected in the public's name at some time or other as being examples of the 'vitally important' or 'cutting-edge' art of its particular era.

Yet, faced by it, one was forced to wonder who on earth could ever have believed that much of this formerly fashionable stuff had any merit at all.

The distinction between fashion-conscious art gallery directors and curators 'buying what was being done' and ambitious artists 'doing what was being bought' was possibly always a fine one yet the evidence continues to remain in such important repositories to remind us of some of the more cautionary consequences of buying what was once held to be highly significant and fashionable art.

Yet perhaps we should recognise here that at least part of the problem of so-called progressive ideas of all kinds is that they seem to attract to themselves a highly favourable yet purely rhetorical language. Thus the trendy but purblind curator could comfort himself with the notion that he at least was squarely on the side of 'brave experiment', 'cutting-edge development' and even of the supposedly inevitable 'evolution' of art itself while any who opposed him were not just likely to be head-in-the-sand reactionaries but may even have been secretly 'seeking to put the clock back'.

How could anyone be that basely reactionary?

Sadly even today too many members of the public are unable to see beyond such elementary misuse and warping of language although happily that does not stop them from suspecting that 'something or other' has been and continues to be wrong with a great deal of the visual art they have been involuntarily obliged to support for decades past through their taxes.

Unusually for a professional art critic I would suggest that 'something or other' really has been wrong with a large part of the whole concept of 'modern' art almost from its first beginnings so that the public's suspicions are, in this instance at least, essentially on the right track.

Indeed, I still tend to blame myself for not realising earlier than I did the paramount importance in all of this of which of its two legitimate meanings we assign to the familiar adjective 'modern'.

Possibly any such subject may strike you at first as merely a minor-seeming semantic quibble.

Yet, as I hope to demonstrate, its consequences could hardly be more far-reaching in the case not just of the visual arts but across the entire spectrum of recent and present artistic activities.

In the latter years of his career my late father helped revise major dictionaries for a living – including the old thirteen volume Complete Oxford English Dictionary. But we do not need such a weighty dictionary here to tell us that the simple adjective 'modern' has two distinctly different meanings. Indeed, the Concise Oxford Dictionary – which was once found in most educated English-speaking households – is sufficient here for our needs.

That handy dictionary tells us that the adjective 'modern' has two discrete meanings: *of the present and recent times* and *new-fashioned not antiquated.*

Fairly obviously the first of these meanings relates simply *to time and period* while the second relates no less evidently *to style and attitude.*

Are we all in agreement so far?

So let us at least kick off our discussion simply by asking ourselves this: when we speak of 'modern' art which of those two definitions springs more rapidly – or indeed automatically – to mind?

In short, does the description 'modern' art simply cover any art at all which was created in the 'modern' period – say during the past 100 years or so?

I do not think that is what most of us understand by the word 'modern' at all in this particular context.

In fact 'modern' art has always defined itself – right from the outset – more or less entirely through its style and attitude.

Such art may admittedly also be 'of the present and recent times' but that is entirely incidental to my argument because it is its stylistic appearance or attitude alone which basically defines it as 'modern'. In other words *formal* novelty has always been the most obviously recognisable characteristic of 'modern' art.

Indeed, it is primarily work which is 'formally novel' which one would expect to find in any of the great many 'museums of modern art' and 'modern art collections' which are scattered in increasingly large numbers across the face of our present-day planet.

Clearly a museum of modern art is thus not simply a showplace or repository for the very best art of the 'modern' period – say of the past 100 or so years – *irrespective of its style* but is basically a showcase instead for often extreme forms of formal novelty.

To the best of my belief no museums or collections of relatively

recent art exist anywhere where the art is not primarily 'formally'
modern in nature.

Have we not therefore made *formal novelty* our effective index of
artistic quality?

Perhaps the next question a reasonable person might therefore ask
is this: who, if anyone, ever decreed that this gross form of apparent
bias against any form of more traditional-looking living art must be
so?

And if they did how on earth could they even begin to justify such
a patently unjust and bizarre-seeming decision?

What some of us may have failed to recognise here is that not just
in all of the arts but in almost all other aspects of our lives two vital
behavioural traditions exist: in short what we could appropriately call
a continuous tradition as well as a radical one. To provide merely one
example of such duality traditional Christian belief clearly belongs
– as a long-established faith – to what could justifiably be called a
'continuous' tradition.

Thus in the case of a 'continuous' artistic tradition an artist would
build upon and refine established practices – which generally first
established themselves through their accepted merits – and may
continue to employ such means until a time may arrive when they
seem inadequate for *some particular and highly individual expressive need* .

I hope you may agree here that it is as well to understand the
scope and merit of any long- established tradition before deciding
peremptorily to abandon it.

It thus seems worth mentioning that in terms of Western painting,
at least, means of depiction which embraced the physical world
known to man and sometimes the metaphysical world of human
imagination provided entirely sufficient scope for the *full expression* of
the unquestionable genius of artists as various as Giotto, Giorgione,
Goya and Gauguin, say, over a period of six centuries.

In other words from about 1300 to 1900, years which likewise
saw the full flowering of the great genius of painters ranging from
van Eyck, Mantegna, Botticelli, Leonardo, Michelangelo, Raphael,

Giovanni Bellini, Titian, El Greco, Holbein, Caravaggio, Rubens, Rembrandt, Velazquez, Vermeer, Tiepolo, Constable, Courbet, Manet and van Gogh – or any other score of more or less incomparable artists from that span of centuries you might personally care to choose – a central, as yet unbroken backbone existed within the body of Western painting which vitalised and inspired all those connected to it.

Many of the artists I have just mentioned were indeed relatively radical within their respective eras while yet remaining within the great, overall tradition which thus simply *contained* rather than necessarily *restricted* them.

The early years of the twentieth century, however, soon saw the fierce and flagrant challenging of all such tradition and it is significant to note here that while readily identifiable 'art movements' were relatively rare in previous centuries, the 20th century alone produced at least *one major, readily identifiable art movement for every two to three years of its entire span.*

In short, how or why did we apparently allow ourselves to become in thrall simply to novelty?

Each novel modern movement would, of course, generally claim to 'extend existing boundaries' and it is hard not to see art here as simply clinging to the coat-tails of technology where 'experimental breakthroughs' often really did and still continue to lead to genuine advances in technological fields such as medicine which, *unlike* art, are thus *genuinely cumulative as well as evolutionary in their basic nature.*

In art, however, the radical tradition has often ironically been more schismatic than cumulative in its effect with art movements frequently claiming to make whatever preceded them either completely 'irrelevant' or 'outmoded'… For example Futurism certainly made just such inflated claims in its overblown-seeming manifesto of 1910.

In many ways, in fact, 'radical' art often dates much faster than any of the art from the continuous tradition which it sought to replace.

Here, indeed, is another ironic subject for reflection.

Often, also, those heavily involved in formally radical early modern movements such as Fauvism and Futurism grew bored themselves with the restrictive nature of their self-imposed modernistic straitjackets.

Although, for some reason, this is generally little remarked on, many modern movements were, in fact. no less proscriptive in their basic nature than the crustiest of academic disciplines of bygone times.

Thus when Braque accused Picasso of 'betraying modernism' in the era following the First World War Braque was revealing precisely such an ideological intolerance. That was because the condition of being avant-garde or modern was looked on by Braque as a form of unquestionable artistic virtue *in itself*...

Similar accusations were also made about other artists as relevant to the history of 20th century art as Andre Derain and Giorgio de Chirico.

Thus at one time even to be seen to flirt with tradition – let alone to embrace its continuing relevance and importance – was once considered by all who regarded themselves as 'true' modernists to be a heresy worthy of instant expulsion from their ranks.

Here, perhaps, we can at last begin to see the great liberating advantage of defining all 'modern' art solely through its period rather than largely by its style.

At a stroke, for example, such a step avoids stylistic proscriptiveness – which has proved one of the worse and more destructive aspects of modernism – and also acknowledges the evident truth that all those working in the modern period are more or less *unavoidably* 'modern' in their *sensibilities* if not necessarily in their chosen modes of working.

Thus you may care to ask yourselves here whether such noted 20th century painters as Edward Hopper, Balthus and Stanley Spencer, say, really were any less 'modern' in their sensibilities than their approximate contemporaries and fellow-countrymen – drawn similarly from America, Switzerland and Britain respectively – Mark Rothko, Paul Klee and Ben Nicholson?

A quick glance at the respective lifetimes of each of these threesomes shows they are at least broadly contemporary. How then can one trio truly be said to be less 'modern' than the other *in any other aspect than choice of artistic expression?*

All six of these painters, I hope you may agree, were artists of very high calibre indeed yet rather significantly one of these trios was happily included in Sir Herbert Read's formerly influential work *A Concise History of Modern Painting* (Thames & Hudson, first published in 1959) while the other – no less significantly – was just as peremptorily excluded.

Astonishingly to me, at least, Read's exclusions were totally deliberate and considered and he attempted – rather feebly – to explain them thus: "I do not deny the great accomplishment and permanent value of the work of such painters as Edward Hopper, Balthus, Christian Berard or Stanley Spencer (to make a random list); they certainly belong to the history of art in our time. But not to the history of the style of painting that is specifically 'modern'…"

I was a young painter at the very outset of my career in 1959 when Read's book was first published and can strongly confirm its huge and lasting influence not least through my own earliest professional experiences. Indeed, at one time it was a standard text-book on most art history courses in British schools and universities.

However, by a strange irony, the reputations both of Paul Klee and Ben Nicholson have subsided markedly since 1959 at which stage Klee's reputation still possibly rivalled that even of Picasso while Ben Nicholson was at that same time quite widely held to be the most important British painter thus far of the 20th century. Undoubtedly that was because of the formally *'advanced'* nature of his semi-abstract art of the time.

So let us consider here, for a moment, the huge extent to which style rather than any other factor formerly influenced artistic reputation.

What we see here, in fact, is that failure to conform to fashionable styles can clearly be extremely damaging professionally. Thus to the best of my belief there are no paintings of significance by either Edward Hopper or Balthus, say, in any British or Australian public collections to this day. Yet both were unquestionably major 20th century painters – as well as ones who were very widely respected not just by the public but also by their professional peers.

Indeed, in terms of providing a descriptive and psychological insight into early 20th century American life some might rank Edward Hopper even with the acclaimed early 20th century American novelist Scott Fitzgerald yet Hopper was still deemed by Read to deserve exclusion from his book solely on the grounds of *personal artistic style.*

I hope you will at least begin to see by now that there is something utterly wrong with such an exclusion.

In short, famous paintings such as *Nighthawks* were essential to the expression of Hopper's personal understanding of modern life.

What I suggest here, in fact, is that to a large extent an officially-endorsed cult of formal novelty effectively poisoned the free development of art in America, Britain and in much of the rest of the Western world including Australia from at least the 1950s onwards with consequences which were not just entirely unnecessary but also deeply damaging to decades of artistic practice.

In short, the cult of often pointless novelty effectively poisoned not just the practice of visual art itself but also those of art education, art criticism and the proper understanding of art history to an extent which will be very hard ever to rectify – even were we to begin right now to acknowledge the full folly and horror of what we have done.

In fact by our failure to insist on a neutral, simply temporal meaning for the word 'modern' we have grossly impoverished – and to a large extent undermined the continuing human relevance of – a very significant proportion of the art of the entire 20th century.

Viewed historically, in short, visual art is too important to human civilisation to be regarded effectively as some kind of faddish intellectual fashion item – but that, very sadly, is what far too much of our recent visual art has essentially become.

*In a letter I wrote which was published in the April edition of *Quadrant* I proposed that the German 20th century artist Lotte Laserstein was possibly the most accomplished female painter of that entire century.

However, if you have pesonally never heard of her do not feel in the least bit diminished because her name did not appear, for example, in what was claimed to be a definitive fairly recent survey of female artists: Whitney Chadwick's *Women, Art and Society* (Thames & Hudson 1990) a work which lists roughly 500 female artists from the past 500 years...

I have a strong suspicion here that Chadwick, who is nevertheless a highly respected American academic, may never even have heard of Laserstein at the time of her book's publication. Probably the particular circumstances of Laserstein's life are to blame.

Lotte Laserstein was born in 1898 in Prussia and due to her rare and precocious talent was one of the first women ever to be admitted to the Berlin Academy of Arts where she rose shortly to the position of Atelier Meisterschuler or 'star pupil' earning herself her own studio and also winning the prestigious gold medal there in 1925. However, simply because she had one Jewish grandparent she was effectively exiled to Sweden in 1937 where she lived for the remainder of a long and productive professional life.

I first saw Laserstein's work in 1987 at a joint exhibition spread over two private galleries in London and instantly recognised its truly remarkable qualities. Indeed I immediately made a strong recommendation that the largest painting in the two shows *The Roof Garden, Potsdam* (111 x 205 cm), which was painted in 1928, should be purchased by the Tate Gallery in London. The painting shows five figures and a dog enjoying a casual meal and drink on a balcony with a vast panorama of Potsdam – subsequently largely destroyed in the Second World War – forming an extremely detailed backdrop to the occasion. I can think of hardly any other 20th century painter – of either gender – who would have been capable of creating such an arresting and impressive historic work.

In the event, the Tate Gallery's Acquisitions Committee under the then chairmanship of world famous modernist architect Richard Rogers – designer of the Pompidou Centre in Paris – declined the purchase on the highly significant grounds that the work was simply not '*modern*' enough for inclusion in the Tate's collection.

I use the foregoing as a more or less perfect example of the deleterious effects of making the adjective 'modern' a 'stylistic' criterion of worth rather than one which relates purely and simply to period.

It may also be thought here that being effectively exiled for life from her homeland -basically through the activities of Hitler – provided Laserstein with a fairly acute awareness of what it was like to live through extremely hazardous 'modern' times.

It is my opinion that the Tate Gallery in London has probably never turned down the chance to acquire a more accomplished or historically interesting painting for public display.

In the meantime that gallery's enormous storerooms remain full to bursting with national and international 'modernist' artistic ephemera which all too often is of the most banal and worthless kind.

What I therefore suggest in conclusion is that the precise meaning we assign to the adjective 'modern' – in artistic terms at least – could hardly be more significant for the present and continuing health of our entire culture.

Quadrant, July/August 2015

33

MODERNISM: AT WAR WITH DELUSION

I was 28 at the time of my first protracted visit to Spain, a country for which I have since formed a deep-rooted affection. In retrospect I cannot but marvel at how little I knew then of any wider world.

My conversion to Rome the previous year, 1962, had certainly helped clarify my thinking – for example through ceasing to view the political and religious history of Europe any longer from an exclusively British or Anglican point of view.

In my professional life as an artist, however, I still found myself tugged this way and that by conflicting theories.

The received wisdom of that time was that an artist living then 'must' try to make modern art – whatever that might be – in much the same way that 'modern' people 'must' live in modern homes, served by state-of-the-art labour-saving devices. Not to do so could well be thought of as 'reactionary'.

What I began to sense then but could not yet articulate fully was the extent to which rhetorical use of language was coming to influence our lives not just in obvious fields such as advertising and politics but also now through art.

I was not destined to begin writing art criticism regularly for more than a decade but what I began to realise was the dangerous extent to which rhetorical use of language had already come to rule contemporary art theory and practice. Slogans already formed an inadequate substitute for considered thought in the minds of many of the younger artists I knew, with the effect that most thought and spoke almost entirely in clichés: "nobody should try to put the clock back" etc.etc.

A depressingly high number of visual artists continue to suffer from the same affliction to this day.

Just one of those clichés was the one I came to look on later on as 'the temporal imperative': in other words an extension of the determinist doctrine that people are somehow compelled to behave in certain ways at given moments of history. But if artists really were so coerced would not that be a total contradiction of one of the central claims of modernism: that it encourages total freedom of thought and practice?

What I describe here is typical of the kind of paradox which troubled me during the evolutionary stages of my thinking about art. However, in common with most people, the greatest barrier to my attainment of greater understanding of art at that stage of my career was simply lack of knowledge. Far too much of my appreciation of painting and sculpture was derived from reading rather than from first-hand acquaintance with the works themselves. At that stage I had seen in the flesh only a small proportion of the works which I imagined wrongly that I 'knew'. Indeed, much of my first-hand knowledge of art was derived in those days from only a few collections – most notably those of the National Gallery in London, the Tate Gallery and the Victoria & Albert Museum.

I suspect that the foregoing provided at least part of the reason why a first visit to the great museum known as the Prado while staying in Madrid had such an overwhelming effect on me. But that was not the sole explanation for what subsequently took place.

Until that moment, at least, I continued to entertain vague notions of being some kind of 'modern' person, thinker and artist. After the beginning of 1963, however, I no longer felt able to wear any such comforting cloak of contemporary being.

One effect of my series of visits to the Prado was to cause me to view the basic notions of artistic time and fashion in a radically different way. Indeed I look back on that now as the true beginning of my artistic education. Regrettably, however, the consequences of such insights tend to prove more beneficial to the quality of one's thinking than to the quality of one's life. By their nature they are more likely to isolate us than otherwise.

Until 1963 I had tended to accept, somewhat thoughtlessly I admit, the very widespread view that contemporary artistic practice was somehow simply our present-day 'equivalent' of that of the major historic eras which preceded it. Thus, however different it might be in its appearance, this notion maintained that the art of Mark Rothko, say, or of Jackson Pollock – two artists who were venerated especially back in 1963 – was simply our contemporary 'equivalent' of the art of masters of the past such as Velazquez and Goya. But a major stumbling-block here was that it resolutely refused to look or to seem 'equivalent'.

Whatever complex excuses one might make for it, the art of such as Rothko and Pollock continued not just to look inferior but also to seem extraordinarily limited in its expressive scope when compared with that of Velazquez and Goya as well as with that of a whole host of even earlier great masters. How, for example, could an artist with Rothko's working methods even begin to comment on the horrors of human conflict in the way Goya had done so forcefully in his unforgettable series of etchings *The Disasters of War*?

Clearly colour alone which was – for a wholly abstract artist such as Rothko – a sole effective vehicle of feeling, was inherently incapable of articulating any comparable weight of metaphysical horror.

To put it briefly, the modernist creed of inevitable evolution and progress seemed to have an insuperable flaw in it which could not be dispensed with easily or at all.

But could it then be that the writings of, say, Clement Greenberg and Patrick Heron – two critics who wielded immense influence in 1963 on either side of the Atlantic – were based on fundamental fallacies? And what about their great armies of followers and fellow travellers who largely dominated official thinking and practice in the arts of the Western world at that time?

Even in terms of numbers alone, surely not all of them could simply be deluded?

If my dilemma seems quaint or even laughable today, it certainly did not seem so at the time. Indeed to think thus would be to discount the degree of influence exerted by modernist thinkers of that era, not least in controlling professional opportunity of all kinds. If dissenting voices did exist they were certainly very seldom heard.

It was extraordinarily cold in Madrid at the time of my visit and the welcoming warmth of the galleries of the Prado may well have been one of the factors which drew me back there late one afternoon as the light began to fade in the streets outside.

The galleries themselves were entirely physically deserted yet I felt a strange sense of presence as though the dead artists whose works graced the walls had summoned me back there to some kind of posthumous parliament.

"If you listen attentively enough, you will learn something of great value" a deep, echoing voice seemed to say almost audibly.

What I grasped in the next moment or moments remains hard to describe.

Suddenly I understood that the 300 years which had passed since the death of Velazquez represented a mere blink of the cosmic eye. As a consequence I no longer felt myself to be part of the art history of any particular age but of all ages and realised simultaneously what a great privilege that was.

Most of us are far too obsessed with our own time and are inclined to dignify it all too often with an excessive and undeserved importance.

Modernism in art had attempted to make a clean break with the past and to impose a new and radical set of values on the rest of us. Yet the great oversight it made was essentially this: great art of all kinds and of all eras is essentially timeless. What it tells us about the human condition never becomes any less relevant or true.

In ceasing to regard myself any longer as a modernist or as someone landlocked by the 20th century or by any of its obsessions I felt utterly liberated suddenly as well as free to make art in future in whatever way I chose.

Unless guns are held to their heads all artists who live outside totalitarian regimes are similarly free.

Unfortunate circumstances such as the latter aside, any compulsion to work in this manner or that is *for all artists of all kinds and at all times* completely illusory.

The demon of supposed artistic progress and evolution is, in fact, merely a particularly cunning disguise for the even less reputable demon of artistic fashion.

Annals, October 2011

34

AT THE SHALLOW END

In the mid-Sixties the young David Hockney must have reflected at times on how easily fame and comparative fortune had come his way. The work with which he first achieved prominence was hardly profound and was characterised, above all, by a somewhat self-conscious stylishness.

Stylishness is what often redeems early and middle-period Hockney, yet is simultaneously a shield and a shortcoming. It is a quality found widely also among leading illustrators and graphic designers. Once developed, it allows effects to be achieved with an apparent effortlessness and absence of agonizing, yet stylishness can also mask inadequate drawing and understanding of the seen.

It is very widely believed that Hockney is a masterly draughtsman. Most of my critical colleagues state this with certainty and the view also has the status of gospel among collectors. This is a major but rather debatable claim and one which the present retrospective exhibition at the Tate Gallery gives us a chance to judge fairly. Where is the evidence of this mastery and with which other artists should we compare him?

Early Hockney paintings from 1960 and 1960 share something of the spontaneity of graffiti and clearly owe much to the French artist Dubuffet. Many possess some degree of informal charm even for those without any particular interest in homosexual relationships. The work which followed developed and improved upon this canon. By 1964, the 26 year-old artist was in California. In the words of his friend and Royal College colleague R.J. Kitaj: "His romance with LA was about two things. Los Angeles was 'elsewhere', about as unlike England as any place could be and, as his friend Christopher Isherwood said about Berlin, Los Angeles meant boys. Together these things spelled romance…"

A number of the better-known paintings which follow feature the putative romance of poolside and shower-room, but does 'Two Boys in a Pool, Hollywood' from 1965 presage any burgeoning mastery? Rather the reverse I would say yet the artist grew steadily in confidence and pictorial ability nevertheless. 'Peter getting out of Nick's Pool' of 1966 and 'A Bigger Splash' of 1967 lift this particular form of stylish image-making and witty observation to a somewhat higher plane, but much of the subsequent popularity of the pool paintings derives simply from their hedonistic subject matter.

However by 1971 the artist was trying his hand at a more direct realism in 'Portrait of an Artist (Pool with Two Figures). But here and in 'Le Parc des Sources, Vichy' of the previous year, the going had become tougher as a consequence. Trees and wooded slopes are not this particular artist's forte and refused resolutely to succumb to simple, stylistic formularisations.

David Hockney appears to be better at coming to terms with inanimate objects, preferably indoors. Simple, recessive space does not always work in his paintings even when intended to do so, Let your gaze wander beyond the windows in 'Mr and Mrs Clark and Percy' from 1970-71, or in 'Henry Geldzahler and Christopher Scott' of 1969. How unconvincing these outdoor worlds are compared with that painted by Lucian Freud in his great double portrait of 1984-85 'Two Irishmen in W11'.

Hockney himself admits the failure: 'From 1969 to 1972 or so I did a number of paintings in a naturalistic style with a very clear one-point perspective…What I wanted to do, what I was struggling to do, was to make a very clear space, a space you felt clear in…Well I just couldn't achieve that clarity frankly; it was a hopeless struggle…'

Not having overcome this particular hurdle, the artist has concentrated subsequently on different forms of space both through photography and frequent invocations of the Cubism of Picasso.

Many hold today that all representation of the seen is dishonest to some extent and Hockney seems obsessed unnecessarily with this issue. One presumes however that he chose voluntarily to be an artist rather than an opthalmist.

The artist has so often, on the whole successfully, been involved in stage design and other projects over the past 15 years that painting has seldom taken absolute precedence. Yet, like many before him who have acquired wealth and popular acclaim, Hockney appears concerned increasingly now about how his art will be perceived in a more serious and long-term context. In the predominantly gloomy artistic climate of the past 30 years, Hockney has been notable for his often endearing panache which may even invite rather unwise comparisons to be made with French painting of the inter-war years.

But Hockney's bright, often lurid palette falls far short of the subtlety of Matisse, who was a consummate colourist. Nor, to make a less obvious but no less valid comparison does Hockney have the brio and deftness of touch of Raoul Dufy, who was a draughtsman of genuine accomplishment. An even less remarked-on shortcoming of Hockney is a general absence of poetry; indeed 'Iowa' 1964 and 'Mt Fuji and Flowers' from 1974 are lyrical rarities. On the whole, the artist's pictorial cleverness is calculated rather than inspired.

What are we to make of the most recent paintings? The 20foot 'Mulholland Drive; the Road to the Studio' seems muddled in intention and execution and a wall of recent portraits is simply clumsy and unappealing. Hockney remains a talented and versatile artist but his reputation as a painter alone rests on rather dubious ground. The glare of publicity which has surrounded him for 25 years should not blind us to the fact that the splash he has made so far has been some distance still from the deeper end of the pool.

The Spectator UK, 8 November 1988

35

WHIMS ANCIENT AND MODERN

My heart sank a little when I learned that Lincoln cathedral was to become the centre of a programme of contemporary art which would extend also to other buildings in the city. If not the loveliest, Lincoln is surely the grandest and most uplifting of Britain's Gothic cathedrals. Last year I was present at an exhibition of often bizarre modern sculpture placed upon the hallowed lawns of Chichester cathedral. The experience was humbling, destroying even for the most hardened any last illusions of 20th century progress.

Before travelling to Lincoln, my instincts warned me that I was in for another spoonful from the same medicine bottle. But this time most of the art on view would not merely be on the lawns of consecrated buildings but within their fabric itself.

The theme of the Lincoln event, so far as I could understand it at all from the reverential rhetoric of the printed publicity, was that modern art is simply another, mysterious aspect of God's great bounty. Sister Wendy Beckett, a contemplative nun and recent embellishment to the ranks of art critics, writes thus in an essay in the glossy catalogue prepared for the exhibition: "Prayer is exposure to the unknown mystery of God. Art demands that we surrender to the unknown power of an artist. We cannot make conditions in advance in either case. Our attitude to prayer and to the art of our times rests on rather similar foundations…Looking at art and looking at God have much in common".

Is there a protocol for disagreeing politely but extremely firmly with a nun? I fear the list of those I offend mortally grows longer year by year. Gilbert and George still remain top of that roll of honour, of course, and one assumes somehow that the good sister might not be too anxious to join their particular company. Her suggested blind leap from reason may be vital, at the last, for spiritual illumination. Generally, however, sound appraisal of the art of our time seems to me to demand less, rather than more blind credulousness.

Not so long ago, an almost total absence of intellectual rigour characterised the practice and criticism of avant-garde art. Terror, inspired by the wrong-minded but brief public rejection of Impressionism, unmanned us utterly so that we clutched all that was new in art, trembling, to our bosoms. In her essay, Sister Wendy reiterates this hoary but largely inaccurate cautionary tale.

What is it then that distinguishes the new role of art in religious and spiritual life from the old? In former times, or so it seems to me, some clear unity of purpose could be discerned at least. Those who built and decorated the great Gothic cathedrals of Europe understood that their artefacts stood for God's greater glory and for the enlightenment and encouragement of their congregations. Thus the purposes of the Stations of the Cross were not merely vague adjurations to save old newspapers or even the trees of the rainforest but rather to contemplate the manner in which humankind had treated its intended saviour. Even modern artists of rare idiosyncrasy from pre-war times, such as Eric Gill, harnessed their considerable talents within the framework of accepted Christian iconography; those who have never done so should make a serious effort to see Gill's Stations of the Cross in Westminster cathedral. However, what is happening at Lincoln is a major departure from such traditions. For a start, artists who have been invited to take part in the Lincoln event may have had little interest in or agreement with Christian principles and thus 'do their thing' largely in response to the ambience of ecclesiastical buildings.

Who, by any stretch of the imagination, might be said to benefit from this? The exhibition brochure is clear, for once, on the possible beneficiaries: "Each age has a responsibility to find new ways of expressing faith and reaching people who feel excluded and distanced in their religious life". Are we approaching here that absurd and divisive ground whereon claims are made that many more teenagers would attend church if only priests could be persuaded to wear rock-and-roll tee-shirts instead of those absurd chasubles? Yet for each such hypothetical teenager there is probably a score of flesh-and-blood Christians who have been saddened unutterably by attempted updatings of their liturgy. For Catholics the replacement of their everyday Latin Mass with a second-class vernacular version provides for me merely one example.

Visitors to Lincoln cathedral will currently encounter two large abstract paintings by Jennifer Durrant, hung below windows in the North and South aisles. By colour and design both would make wonderful patterns for ultra-modern rugs, yet neither could really be said to offer any hope to the ecclesiastically disenchanted. Hard by these, a series of five expensive-looking copper panels bear identical minimal motifs in black and white. But is their message to the spiritually distanced similarly clear-cut? By contrast, the large slate circle contributed by Richard Long and an alternative altar by Richard Devereux seem to look back, with a certain nostalgia, to pre-Christian times.

Are we being asked to mourn the passing of the Druids – noted persecutors of early Christians – or merely the demise of a 'healthier' ancient pantheism? Apparently the gold leaf which is all that covers Leonard McComb's 'Portrait of a Young Man Standing' was at least one leaf too few for the sensibilities of one of Lincoln's deans.

Probably other exhibits caused less embarrassment merely because merit and meaning were less approachable.

The ruins of the Bishop's Palace contain, among other things, aesthetically pleasing but purely organic sculpture by Peter Randall-Page, attractive nods in the direction of Eastern faiths in the prayer sticks of Eileen Lawrence plus a vast, wax-covered floor, brainchild of Glen Onwin, who hopes that moulds and crystals may flourish therein. Is this a metaphor for Christian growth and renewal? Or rather for rot and decay? To Christians who are still oppressed brutally for their faith in other lands, the agonised goofiness of Britain's Anglican church must sometimes take some crediting.

The Spectator UK, 21 July 1990

36

FAITH-KILLING FURNITURE

A first effect of war is to banish complacency. All of a sudden morality and mortality seem a little bit less abstract and remote. Unsurprisingly artists who go through war often discover unexpected changes in their priorities when peace returns. For the first time in years the artist may see beauty even in a run-down local park. By contrast convoluted intellectual theories of art may seem a touch less compelling suddenly.

If danger and deprivation heighten a sense of the real then peace and plenty possibly erode it. Today the Saatchi Collection makes a fitting monument to a time of economic boom and to the financial profligacy that accompanied it.

Perhaps that is one reason why going to the Saatchi Collection has provided some of the more unreal moments of my life. Another may be the strange atmosphere of secrecy and security that surrounds the collection; even something as straightforward as the telephone number there turns out to be ex-directory. Ask a taxi driver to take you to the huge premises that house the collection and he will generally disclaim any knowledge of its whereabouts although it has been open now for over five years. The last driver to take me there was even willing to bet that the address I had given him was wrong since he claimed to know that whole area particularly well. Usually the spiked steel gates which bar the way to the collection are closed. Indeed, like the similarly unmarked doors to lavatories within the building itself they seem unwilling to disclose either name or purpose.

The trio of artists currently on view there consist of the Americans Richard Artschwager and Cindy Sherman and the Englishman Richard Wilson. The art of the first and last falls broadly into the category of objects which those who possess most things on earth already might just conceivably covet. Artschwager began his professional life in 1949 as a furniture maker. More lately he has switched to parodying furniture but calling his product art. Some of that on view is based on ecclesiastical examples: altarpieces, lecterns, confessionals. However, the artist constructs his borrowed artefacts in materials of peculiarly disagreeable colour and appearance. But this, so the exhibition catalogue tells us, is 'a brilliant acerbic act of nihilism…through embodying artifice (lack of truth), it also casts doubt on religious conviction and the power of ritual objects to offer solace. This one decision sets up exquisite tension, meaning and form that gives all subsequent work the ironic potential of parody'.

I hate to contradict a professional colleague of course but feel the precise way an altar constructed from formica can cast doubt on anything at all, other than its owner's judgement perhaps, is something less than obvious. Moreover, I imagine that within the walls outside the Saatchi Collection at least 'religious conviction and the power of ritual objects to offer solace' may shortly prove in greater rather than lesser demand – to the severely wounded on recently opened battlefields for instance. In the meantime, one's sense of relevance, let alone of reality, is hardly advanced by the knowledge that Mr.Artschwager is accustomed to 'wearing a pullover decorated by a flight of ducks'. 'The birds' so the catalogue note continues 'seem to have evacuated the heavens for relocation on the artist's chest'.

One rather hopes that is all they evacuated.

Regrettably, the same written source does not disclose how Richard Wilson attires himself, but since one of his artistic materials is sump oil, one somehow imagines he does so less fancifully. Some gallery-goers may have met Mr.Wilson's famous oil-slick before, though some fresh topicality could be argued now in its favour. The visual illusion it creates by reflection is a clever one. Those who know the installation of old will need no enjoining not to put their hands over the side of the walkway which protrudes out into the oily lagoon. Paper towels are provided for those who are less familiar or wary. Indeed a handful of these might help dry the eyes of those less than overcome by the nature of Mr.Wilson's remaining exhibits: the frame of a greenhouse halted while passing through a gallery wall and the apparent remains of a touring caravan. Perhaps you may even find such artistic objects yourself at the unexplored end of your garden?

The third exhibitor is Cindy Sherman, a young woman who, perhaps lacking a doll when young, took to dressing herself up instead. She has managed to make a successful artistic career subsequently from this unusual habit. Make-up, masks and a malleable face help her disguise her features still further. The results of her disguise are then recorded photographically, sometimes even poignantly. However, we learn from the exhibition's reliably remarkable catalogue that since 1983 'the nice girl no longer seems willing to solicit masculine approval'. Indeed 'she is not content after all to be a dreamy mirror for masculine fantasy. The following series explore madness, depravity, ugliness and disease…misshapen faces are covered in warts, breasts and buttocks in weeping pustules…'

Male cynics may reflect here that some women will go to almost any lengths to get themselves noticed.

The Spectator UK, 26 January 1991

37

MANY A BOSOM BARED

Less than a quarter of my way round *The Last Romantics* the vast show on view currently at the Barbican, this week's headline swam effortlessly into my consciousness and lodged there immovably.

I intend no self-congratulation in suggesting it would make a more apt and accurate title for the exhibition itself.

Romantic has become one of the new rallying cries of those bored with an exclusively modern reading of the history of art in the past 100 years. However, considerable danger is courted now by deliberate or unwitting misuse of the term romantic. The Romantic movement formed one of the great thrusts of European as well as of British art and I would be among the first to defend its principles. The movement began in the 18th century as a reaction to scientific empiricism and the Age of Reason. Its precise parameters may be inexact but one had not foreseen previously the likelihood of so strong an identification of the word with what amounts largely to romantic whimsy.

I am appalled by this particular development, for the full title of the exhibition, *The Last Romantics: the Romantic Tradition in British Art, Burne-Jones to Stanley Spencer* appears quite specific. We are not dealing in short with some random agglomeration of artefacts chosen purely from personal liking, but with an exhibition that one might expect to be a visual demonstration of its title. No doubt the choice of such titles is a crucial factor in attracting public response. The present one is taken from a poem by Yeats: 'We were the last romantics – chose for theme/Traditional sanctity and loveliness.' The poetic source is not especially important and will remain unknown, in any case, to most of those who visit the show.

I have taken issue in recent years with the growing inaccuracy of the titles of major exhibitions of a public nature, but the present naming seems misleading to an unprecedented degree. From the title the inescapable impression is given that we are dealing with the last exponents of romantic art in Britain who died out apparently with Stanley Spencer. What is really on view, however, is a selection mostly of narrative painting illustration, printmaking and sculpture from the years 1880-1940, some of it of very doubtful merit beginning with the works of the pivot of the exhibition himself, Edward Burne-Jones. I strongly question whether any of the Pre-Raphaelites belong to the true Romantic tradition, least of all the man who led them into final decline.

As a major protagonist of Burne-Jones the originator of the present exhibition, John Christian, seems as blind to the artist's faults as he is confused about the entire history of romantic art.

Words such as romantic must retain some agreed and reasonable meaning if we are not to be plunged into semantic and art-historical chaos. In his worthy book on neo-Romantic art in Britain, Dr.Malcolm Yorke writes: "As a cultural phenomenon English Romanticism might be said to begin around 1780 when Blake first exhibited at the new Royal Academy. By 1840, when Victoria came to the throne, its strength had passed... Even though Turner was still alive and creating his astonishing late works English art in general by 1850 was well down its slide into the emptily picturesque, mawkish anecdotalism, border-to-border symbolism and exotic trifles – all weaker by-products of the vigorous Romanticism that had gone before."

I heartily agree.

John Christian's avowed aim was simply to span the gap in time between the works of the Pre-Raphaelites, as exemplified by the popular Tate Gallery exhibition from 1984, and those of the neo-Romantics subject of that stimulating show, *A Paradise Lost*, presented at the Barbican in May 1987. One problem arising from this aim is that Mr Christian was led thereby to exclude Graham Sutherland and John Piper, who were not only central to the latter exhibition but vital also to the true romantic revival of the Thirties and beyond. I am sure the name of Henry Moore would not have been discussed in this connection yet he, too, was far closer to the romantic spirit exemplified by such as Blake, Palmer, Cotman, Calvert, Ward, Bonington, Constable and Turner, all of whom stood head and shoulders above anyone included in the present show with the exception of Stanley Spencer.

Coming almost at the last, to Spencer's two superb early paintings 'Zacharias and Elizabeth' and 'The Nativity' I could hardly suppress a shout of relief.

There are 557 works altogether and by the time one has walked past a good few acres of damsels tiptoeing in and out of diaphanous nighties, seashells, bathtubs and rosy bowers my sympathies began to lie increasingly with the sea serpents, dragons and other scaly ne'er-do-wells who were assailing them. According to this misplaced conception of romanticism, the baring of one or more breasts was clearly *de rigueur* for pastimes such as archery, needlework, listening to music or merely waiting for (k)night to fall. Few of these maidens look convinced by their chances, more lose some than winsome one is tempted to say. Juno's comely attendant in Waterhouse's 'Echo and Narcissus' made the fatal mistake, repeated so often by package tourists, of not ignoring young Greek men lying about near pools. She has cause to look anxious.

I do not suggest that there was anything wrong with the painterly abilities of Waterhouse or the likes of John Melhuish Strudwick, J.R. Spencer Stanhope, Evelyn de Morgan, Herbert James Draper or Thomas Cooper Gotch. Even some of the less exotically named artists could paint like angels. The objection is that so many did, in fact, paint angels – when they were not painting fairies, witches, swains, sirens and the like in *mélanges* of the mythic, mystic and mediaeval. To borrow from Clive James, many of these images 'grip you like a marshmallow'. The exhibition catalogue devotes a large section to fairyland.

While the show displays the abilities of major illustrators such as Rackham and Dulac, it reminds us that many painters too could show up better in a smaller medium: the woodcuts, drawings and etchings especially of Strang ,Shannon, Robertson, Russell Flint and Edward Frampton are among the best things on view. Often lack of colour adds to rather than diminishes mystery: James Guthrie's tiny etching 'Clouds' has an intensity of vision lacking in so many of the large, vapid, formal paintings. Burne-Jones's 'Vespertina Quies' and Simeon Solomon's 'Love in Autumn' contain passages either of poor painting or sub-standard restoration, while Cecile Walton's 'Suffer Little Children to Come Unto Me' reminds one of nothing so much as Walt Disney. A far truer understanding of the continuing romantic tradition in British art from the inter-war years might have been provided by the inclusion of such as Ravilious, Bawden, Frances Hodgkins and Algernon Newton.

What a relief they would have provided from the elfin pool.

The Spectator UK, 18 February 1989

38

TOE-NAILS OF SOCIALIST SAINTS

With the crash of walls and governments in Eastern Europe reverberating in our ears, the timing of the exhibition *The Rodchenko Family Workshop* at the Serpentine Gallery in London may seem inopportune or even bizarre. Rodchenko, together with his wife Stepanova and such luminaries as Tatlin, El Lissitzky and Malevich, belongs properly to that utopian stage of world communism which antedates the pessimistic but percipient prognostications of writers such as George Orwell and Arthur Koestler. Darkness at noon had yet to arrive because they were still then at the dawning.

I must admit to a deep distrust of utopianism of all kinds, not because I am cynical but because utopianism so often and willfully disregards that essential element called human nature.

Social experiment, if one really must have it, needs to be based on some more profound understanding of the nature of mankind if it is to avoid ending in murderous disaster. Thus, while earnest socialists continue to revere Tatlin's infamous *Monument to the Third International* as an icon, I prefer to see it rather as a headstone commemorating folly. That many of the artefacts displayed in *The Rodchenko Family Workshop* also have the status of sacred relics of socialism was apparent in the drop-jawed mien of many of the visitors to the Serpentine. A friend with whom I viewed the exhibition remarked that much of the show seemed more concerned with polemic than with perception. Of course, much the same might be said of displaying, say, one or more toe-nails of a Christian saint. Yet there at least we are quite clear that our response need not be aesthetic.

To the left-wing faithful the early work of such as Rodchenko reflects the true ideals of communism, untainted as yet by the *realpolitik* of a Lenin or Stalin. In his *The Story of Modern Art* the art historian Norbert Lynton wrote about the era: 'Weakened by international war, by the effects of revolution and civil war, and then also by the war against foreign troops sent to undo the Revolution, Soviet Russia could not but assess every activity by asking whether it secured the Revolution and strengthened the state'. In short, art had to serve the needs of political orthodoxy. Yet Rodchenko occupies a particularly exalted place also in the art historical 'orthodoxy' of modernism: 'A Moscow exhibition of September 1921…included three paintings by Rodchenko that probably ceased to exist many years ago but have become historic…Rodchenko showed three monochrome paintings, *Pure Red Colour, Pure Blue Colour* and *Pure Yellow Colour,* together he named them 'The Last Painting' and announced the death of abstract art'.

Here I should admit that art interests me principally as a visual, aesthetic and spiritual experience. On the whole, avant-gardist gestures fail to engage the viewer in any of those areas. In effect, such gestures have become icons of a peculiarly suffocating orthodoxy inflicted on us by modern art historians. Above all, theirs is a creed of time-worship.

Indeed, in answer to the question 'Why should a pure red or pure blue canvas engage us in the slightest?' what else can the modern art historian reply but 'Because it was painted in this or that year'. Perhaps it is salutary to reflect sometimes that the nine great canvases of Andrea Mantegna's 'Triumphs of Caesar'', which reside today in Hampton Court Palace, were painted in the last 15 years of the 15th century. How dare we write of progress and development in the face of such evidence?

Yet evidence has never deterred the modern art historian in any way, of course. Indeed, here is another wonderful piece of modern art history from the catalogue of the current Serpentine exhibition:

"In December 1915 Malevich had launched Suprematism at the 0.10 exhibition in Petrograd. There he showed *The Black Square* and numerous Suprematist paintings comprising geometric shapes in primary colours painted on white grounds. The ferment of new art infected the younger artists like Rodchenko and Stepanova *who were inspired to take such devlopments further...*

What we are witnessing at the Serpentine seems to me largely an exhibition of the toe-nails of socialist saints. That communism and its turgid orthodoxies should appear to be in some disarray at the precise moment when an exhibition promoting the view that 'the new work that artists were undertaking suggested that art could play a major role in the transformation of society and the creation of a communist environment' is merely an unfortunate historical coincidence.

Transnational exhibitions and their catalogues are months or years in preparation. How would a present-day Muscovite worker respond to the ideals of Rodchenko and others in helping to design a 'workers' paradise' when 70-odd years after the revolution such a worker cannot buy a bar of soap, for example, or almost anything else in Russia's capital?

Some paradise.

Having 'killed' abstract painting by his gesture of 1921, Rodchenk launched himself into typography and advertising, poster, furniture, costume and fabric design, photography and film-making. He also continued to paint in the now familiar Soviet artist's plethora of styles. Are any of his paintings of any great aesthetic merit, as distinct from purely historical interest? I fear the answer is no. This is hardly surprising, perhaps, from a member of a group that styled themselves as 'productivists' and whose studios were renamed 'workshops'. Art itself under any guise they denounced as an anachronism embodying bourgeois values...' How that tired and tendentious rhetoric limps on. Rodchenko seems to me to have had more genuine talent as a photographer than as a painter. His 'production suits' in the meantime have clearly had some major influence on the costume designers for *Star Trek*.

What greater epitaph could one wish?

I cannot help wondering whether the Nineties may at last be the decade when we cease to be hypnotized by so-called art history and demand once more some measure of majesty and presence from our artists?

The Spectator UK, 6 January 1990

39

EVIDENCE OF THE EYES

So, naturalists observe, a flea
Hath smaller fleas that on him prey;
And these have smaller fleas to bite 'em.
And so proceed ad infinitum.
(Jonathan Swift, On Poetry)

Facing recent American art for the second week running gives me an overwhelming itch to find a way back to more solid artistic ground: to the very first flea, as it were.

Confronted at the Saatchi Gallery with the art of such as Basquiat, Borofsky, Haring, Gober and Schnabel it is hard not to conclude that far from circumnavigating seas of portentousness and intellectual manure, American art is immersed deeply – and probably inextricably now – in both.

That the art looks awful, on the whole, goes without saying; the year is 1993 and most are inured utterly by now to art's disagreeable appearance. For those who retain some sympathy or who can be bothered, an ocean of printed material exists to prove this is how everything has to be. Thus the historical evidence adduced by those chosen to write the catalogue essays for *American Art in the 20th Century* is presented as ineluctable. But those who prefer to trust the evidence of their eyes will believe nothing of the sort.

Before or after visiting the Saatchi Gallery, spend an hour at London's National Gallery. Contemplate if you will the wonderful art and complex iconography of the Wilton Diptych made by humankind some 600 years ago. Or cast an eye over Rembrandt, Veronese and

El Greco. It is impossible not to conclude from such observations that the modernist arguments advanced for the art of Schnabel, say, at Saatchi, or Rosenquist and Warhol at the Royal Academy contain some terrible and ultimately implausible flaw.

But, like Swift's first flea, this first bears by now on its back a vast superstructure of lesser lies. We have to see a way somehow past these if we hope to identify the original culprit. As I wrote once about Pravda, the numbers of lies, evasions and half-truths printed does not matter at the last, because these cannot affect the truth of what has happened one iota. Thus whatever the success once claimed in the USSR for five or ten year agricultural plans, peasants in the countryside still knew for sure they were starving.

So it is with recent American art. The stomachs and hearts of aware gallery-goers warn them that they are being offered unsatisfying fare.

Regrettably, transatlantic art critics – with few honourable exceptions – are not up to explaining why this is so to an American audience. Many believe by now that American criticism plays an integral part in the perpetuation of the myth. Indeed, many American critics seem to be employed simply for the contributions they make to national aggrandisement however much this actiivity may conflict with the forming of truer art historical perspectives. In short those who go to the Saatchi Gallery to see American art from 1970 to the present day are advised not to set their expectations too high.

Happily quite the reverse applies to an unsung show of American prints at the Fine Art Society, an institution which often provides a rock of sanity amid fast-rising cloacal seas. American Prints includes American artists of genuine importance to the history of that nation's culture such as John Marin, John Sloan, George Bellows, Grant Wood and Milton Avery, all of whom the Rosenthal/Joachimides axis – the selectors of *American Art in the 20th Century* – chose to ignore. Among a series of visual treats, Edward Hopper's The Cat Boat and Night Shadows stand out, the former for its brilliant rendering of space through the unlikely medium of etching, the second as an image as archetypal of interwar America as Scott Fitzgerald's The Great

Gatsby.

At the Serpentine Gallery we encounter Agnes Martin who is included also in the current American survey. In my hearing a visitor to the show described her paintings at the former venue as resembling 'pyjama materials for convicts'. This is harsh since some look at least equally suitable for the shirts of businessmen. But what is it that we are really witnessing? Paintings of the ineffable, no less. Once again we are asked by apologists to suspend belief in what our eyes apprehend and to float away, in the face of her art, on clouds of semi-consciousness. Whether one could achieve this better or worse in a gallery which was entirely empty at the time of my visit is possibly a moot point.

Although Martin's works may appear austere to visitors, this is not their stated intention. The artist was born in 1912, gave up painting once, moved to New Mexico and now embraces Far-Eastern mysticism. Regrettably, the interview with her published in the exhibition catalogue and her own written notes fail to help close the gulf between what we see before us and her stated intentions. I fear this is not simply because her ideas are poorly expressed but because a number are very firmly rooted in artistic fallacies.

The Spectator, October 2 1993

40

TYCOON'S BUZZ

Why is Mr.Charles Saatchi apparently an obsessive collector of modern art?

I am afraid that why many people behave as they do must remain one of life's more unnerving mysteries. Indeed, why a very large audience of outwardly intelligent people sat through the whole of the Walter Neurath Memorial Lecture delivered at Senate House very recently by famous feminist art historian Griselda Pollock is a puzzle which will go on haunting me for the rest of my life.

As I wandered the whited acres of Mr. Saatchi's shrine to new art, a brilliantly converted paint factory in Boundary Road, NW8 last week, surveying his latest acquisitions (*Young British Artists*) no obvious answer presented itself to explain his actions. Someone suggested to me once that it must be the power to choose which talentless artist to elevate to heights of modish fame that appeals to him. To possess a godlike power to make random interventions into human affairs may well have some attraction but I do not think this is the answer. Looking about me at mounds of mouldering blowflies and such, the pleasure of ownership, in any ordinary sense, seems a fairly unlikely explanation also. Nor is any consistent taste, other than for novelty perhaps, readily discernible in Mr. Saatchi's vast range of purchases. Some regard him as a shrewd businessman whose sheer weight of spending has influenced the market. Others see him more kindly as our sole American-style patron who shows concern for an avant-garde which is neglected cruelly otherwise by the beastly British.

Since I know Mr.Saatchi slightly, though largely as a tennis player, the easiest solution might be to ask him the nature of the buzz he gets from buying entire exhibitions of modern art simply by telephoning him. But as he is reputedly shy and ill at ease with the press – on this particular subject at least – to do so could seem like an unjustified intrusion.

Travelling home from Mr. Saatchi's remarkable gallery, replete with its latest example of ichthyolatry – a tiger shark in a tank – and other putrefying phenomena, my eye lit by chance on the main story in *The Evening Standard*. Although its subject was the Duchess of York, the insight it provided may well account not just for Mr. Saatchi's eccentric-seeming behaviour but that of many of the artists he collects. *The Evening Standard*'s story was of the apparent rift between the Duchess and advisers to royalty within Buckingham Palace, the cause being the former's feckless-seeming behaviour. Oddly, instead of exhorting the Duchess to act more circumspectly, the Palace has preferred to plump for a public relations palliative. In short, image rather than duty was perceived as the crux of the problem. Indeed, no matter how indifferently the Duchess might behave, the trick was to persuade the rest of us to believe otherwise.

Those with memories of any length will recall that Mr. Saatchi's own background – and the basis of his fortune and princely levels of patronage – is the wonderful world of publicity, wherein if a product or service can be presented plausibly enough the pounds and pfennigs will positively leap from our pockets.

Much of Mr. Saatchi's business fame rests on his erstwhile company's successful presentation of the Conservative Party. But would not his company and all the skilled minds it employs have been just as happy selling political parties of some other hue, provided only that the colour of their money was essentially correct? Publicity is a realm in which skills are for hire and wherein personal beliefs of any kind can prove inconvenient impediments. How many covert socialists were obliged to work on the Conservative Party account? Publicity is a force which not only makes some things happen – increased sales of baked beans and hairspray – but makes others appear to happen: an amelioration in the Duchess of York's sense of responsibility for instance.

If the good journalist's world is one of fact, the good advertising man's is one of fancy. The latter's aim is to elide reality and illusion to an extent where they gradually become indistinguishable in the minds of consumers. This kind of mental manipulation does not happen only in consumer societies of course. It is also standard practice for propagandists in every type of totalitarian regime: one has only to think of the poor citizens of the USSR who seldom got the chance to consume anything. But all the countless pages of lies printed in *Pravda* could never really affect the truth of what happened one iota. As the Soviet regime has crumbled away, the truth of its cruelty, corruption and inefficiency stands exposed like a reef at low tide. The true grimness of the Soviet regime was known for all the years of its existence, of course, to all the people who suffered under it. We may pride ourselves on our freedoms in democratic countries, yet yield unwittingly to such intellectual tyrannies as political correctness, feminism and modernism which rely for their influence similarly on methods of mass persuasion rather than on reasoned argument.

Mr.Saatchi seems happy enough to play the role of the inspired collector of avant-garde art. Many believe him to be an enigmatic encourager of genius in others because they have read this frequently in the newspapers. Regrettably, I feel the distinctions between the real and the apparent may no longer be clear even to Mr. Saatchi himself. I blame this on his former profession. Of the tests I would apply to establish a wealthy connoisseur, Mr.Saatchi qualifies only in wealth and willingness, for I cannot discern any pattern or particular inspiration in his buying. More to the point, as the sole mover now in forming the collection that bears his name he seems unable and unwilling to explain its aims, leaving that task to the doubtful competence of others. Few do a plausible or even an intelligible job. Langlands and Bell, exhibitors in the collection's current show, attract the following language in a reprint handed me by the collection's publicity department:

This repetition involves what henceforth shall be called the logic of the again and anew. Marking out a co-presence which is never a simple presence. Not simple because, as will be suggested, the origin is diremptive: anoriginally diremptive…

In flight from such language I turned to a text by the ever-articulate Andrew Graham-Dixon, art critic for *The Independent*, describing work by another of the show's youthful exhibitors:

The fact that the Shark appears to move contributes to its considerable power as an object of contemplation. It is a paradox made solid, this creature, at once frighteningly dynamic and completely still. It is, of course, a vanitas, albeit of an unusual kind: a work of art that prompts reflections on death, its inevitability and our habit of avoiding that most unsavoury and basic fact of our existence…

Those who saw only a slowly decomposing shark in a tank of formaldehyde need not rush either to their opticians or psychiatrists, since Mr.Graham-Dixon is merely describing a personal reaction. I must confess that neither the shark in a tank, which is not a work of art, nor another of this particular young man's creations, *One Thousand Years* (blowflies, maggots, cow's head, insectocutor etc.) which is not a work of art either, prompted any thought of death in me, unless it be by boredom. Nor are the rows of cabinets full of discarded pills and potions, by the same artist, works of art, though they may cause other critics than I to contemplate anything from haemorrhoids to hot flushes.

One of the major purposes of what was once considered a sound education is that it dissipates the attractions exercised by superficial thinking and writing: its recipient is encouraged to learn how to think clearly. Calmness and clarity of thought are the most potent weapons for cutting through inflated claims of any kind, whether they are found in advertising copy, art reviews or feminist oratory.

A basic interest in and instinct for the truth arms us against hustling of all kinds. A person so armed may never be particularly popular or powerful and would probably prefer to end up on the side of angels rather than of Engels. Such a person is never a member of a modish mob.

The current exhibition at the Saatchi Collection purports to introduce the brightest of young British hopefuls to an admiring audience. The first time I was told about the most publicity-conscious of their number I understood his name to be Damian Hearse. As possessor of what Andrew Graham-Dixon describes as 'a single-minded morbidity', Mr.Hirst should at least consider my recommendation for a new surname. The college at which he studied – Goldsmith's – trains its young artists in the manipulation of publicity. Clearly Mr.Hirst has absorbed his lessons very well and is already a minor star of the avant-garde firmament in consequence. Mr.Saatchi like Graham-Dixon cannot but see more in Mr Hirst's festering displays than I do. Possibly both hope to discover the meaning of life from contemplation of foetid fish and fly-blown skulls. I should admit here that if I were seeking a philosophical guru, I doubt I would be scouring the ranks of immature former art students – but then my taste in art seems a bit different from theirs too.

What of the other exhibitors? John Greenwood also seeks to say something significant, but through surrealist similes. His complex organic constructions are drawn and painted carefully and may well be autobiographical: metaphors for romantic mishaps in bedsit land. Alex Landrum, by contrast, paints single-colour canvases which conceal quite cleverly the names given by the manufacturer to the household paints he uses. The process he uses resembles simple blind-embossing but moves the critic Sarah Kent who has written the catalogue to ecstasies of philosophizing: 'The proportions of his canvases are derived from old master paintings so as, subliminally, to affirm their status as artworks…'

Why do Mr. Saatchi's exhibitions encourage even semi-respectable art critics to gush like geysers?

There is so little satisfaction or sense to be extracted from so many of the works on view that it seems to me an attempt is made to obscure their shortcomings in clouds of verbal steam. Mr.Saatchi is a shrewd and successful man with apparent ambitions to be remembered as something more. For my part, I hope he will emerge one day from his veil of vapours and swarm of sycophants to create an achievement of real rather than simulated substance.

The Spectator UK, 4 April 1988

41

POLKE IN THE EYE

To be frank a trip to the Saatchi Collection is seldom an experience to which I look forward with unqualified enthusiasm. On the day of my most recent visit, small black clouds formed a scarabaeoid procession along the St.John's Wood skyline. The massive grey steel gates at 98A Boundary Road, NW8 blocking access to the converted paint factory which houses the Saatchi Collection, set a Kafkaesque tone for any excursion there. Inside the gates, the long bare galleries are windowless and disorientating. If art police existed who might wish to brainwash us into orthodoxy, or otherwise subvert our critical thinking, one feels this is where one might meet them… 'Herr Direktor would like to see you before you go, Mr.Auty, to discuss some of your previous reviews of the collection. You will find it does not pay to think art criticism can be humorous.'

The four artists on show at present – Golub, Guston, Polke and Shapiro – are a relatively cheerless quartet. I do not seek to question the sincerity of any of them but remark in passing, that the automatic equating of grimness with significance suggests too facile a standpoint. The vast paintings by Leon Golub are of mercenaries and prisoners, forming rather stilted tableaux of imminent torture and mayhem.

The subject is moving in itself but I cannot say that Golub makes it any more real for me. Is one supposed to enjoy or even comment on the way the paint is applied when dealing with such depressive subject matter? The glorious conception and handling of Mantegna's *Crucifixion*, for instance, from around five centuries ago, certainly aid both our imagination and understanding. By contrast Golub shuns the directly narrative while flirting simultaneously with a kind of flattened formalism; such factors identify him as a modern painter, of course, yet seem to militate against effectiveness in treating his chosen subject matter.

Such reservations about Golub's methods are unlikely to affect the height of his current international standing. Since, as an American, his work is relatively unfamiliar in Britain, we are indebted to the Saatchis for the opportunities they afford us here to see major displays of work by some of the more visible planets of the current post-modernist galaxy.

Inclusion in the Saatchi Collection must be viewed, in itself, by many as a major step up the ladder of putative fame.

Similarly, Sigmar Polke is not necessarily an artist on whom I would be spending my disposable millions but, once more, the Saatchis have invested heavily. The East German Polke shared the major prize with our own Frank Auerbach at the last-but-one Venice Biennale. By being eclectic, ugly, cryptic and careless-looking, Polke's paintings answer many of the more important canons proposed by the kind of critics who judge international art prizes.

Reading the catalogue for an exhibition of works by Polke, Warhol and Beuys held in Milwaukee and Houston last year, I learn 'There is, as well, the 'cult of personality' surrounding Polke. As in the case with Warhol, and with Joseph Beuys, much has been made of the aura of the artist himself as a potentially supernatural persona.'

Is it some kind of winged being, one wonders, that Sigmar Polke may imminently become? Polke, like the late Joseph Beuys, has certainly gained guru status in the world of recent art. However, visitors may find that whatever course of action or philosophy Polke may be preaching from on high will not be readily apprehensible from the paintings on view. The message, if any, might be thought to be that chaos reigns now on this planet, beyond even such obvious areas as the world of art.

Polke's productions might easily be understood as the work of many, ranging from comic-book figuration to marks which might be described, not unreasonably, as Polke dots and dashes. The artist borrows from historical sources, parodies and makes slighting references, all measures likely to appeal to the weary appetites of modern art historians. Like Julian Schnabel, Polke has been proposed as a contemporary artist of primary importance. Mere looking at his work is most unlikely to reveal why.

Guston, the third of the current quartet, is an artist who has enjoyed something of a reincarnation. Formerly a famed and rather elegant abstractionist of a kind likely to provoke the well-known comment 'there's less in this than meets the eye' Guston became weary and finally apostate. Rejecting the holy aestheticism of paint for paint's sake, he has painted subsequently to find out if the activity remains worth doing at all. One large image 'Painter in Bed' featuring a giant lumpish head, cigarette and liverish eye, might suggest to most people that it isn't. With Guston one buys not simply a bloated, despairing image but a potted history of recent artistic chaos and wrong-mindedness.

The last of the four artists, Shapiro, introduces a touch of levity to a generally dispiriting experience. His sculpture employs an odd, sometimes miniscule scale to explore personal disenchantment, but I did enjoy one precariously balanced figure which refused resolutely to fall flat on its face.

In the context of an exhibition such as this one is desperate to find some glimmer of hope in anything.

The Spectator UK, 6 August 1988

42

IN THE PRESENCE OF GENIUS

For me, one major effect of looking at Velazquez's paintings is the way those of other artists from almost any other period pale by comparison. Wonderful breadth, colour and all-round painterly brilliance alert us that we are in the presence of great genius. Which artists can live with Velazquez at his finest? Rembrandt, Titian and Veronese perhaps but, at most, only a handful of others. Interestingly, Velazquez himself was not an admirer of Raphael.

By chance, Velazquez and the Prado Museum where his work is showing at the moment played a vital formative role in my own artistic growing-up. Trying to describe an experience which occurred in the Prado back in 1963, I wrote later…'the main galleries, being almost empty at the time, exuded a strangely mellow and sepulchral air as the winter daylight faded rapidly in the streets outside. Standing there, I felt an extreme stillness as though I had entered some very Holy Place of Painting where the spirits of dead painters might almost speak to me if I listened attentively enough. Why, all of a sudden, did every argument for the art of the 20th century seem so completely inadequate in the face of Velazquez?'

Had I not been in Madrid very recently to see the current exhibition of some 79 masterworks by Velazquez I am sure the very fine paintings of Wright of Derby would have looked less wrong to me when I saw them at the Tate Gallery on the evening of my return to London.

Velazquez was and is the pinnacle who points up the shortcomings of others. In the face of his paintings, the straightforward language of qualitative comparisons becomes appropriate once more. For instance, what 19 year old ever painted a more remarkable work than Velazquez's *Old Woman Frying Eggs* – one of the first paintings one encounters at the current, unrepeatable exhibition at the Prado?

Like another prodigy, Turner, Velazquez began his training, in his case as an apprentice to an established artist, from a very early age. Velazquez was just 11 when he arrived at the studio of Francisco Pacheco in 1610. By 1617 he had served his apprenticeship and could set up as an artist in his own right. Whilst we may wonder at the precise nature of the system of early 17th century training that Velazquez underwent, there was clearly a lot to be said for it judged simply by results.

On the other hand, Velazquez seems to have possessed great natural ability from the outset. Manet described him aptly as 'le peintre des peintres'.

Like his 19th century French successor, Velazquez was fundamentally a realist, saving most of his powers of invention for the practice of painting itself. Thus he was not a pictorial inventor in the manner of Rubens; his fairly early paintings of mythological and Old Testament subject matter, 'The Forge of Vulcan' 1630 and 'Joseph's Bloody Coat brought to Jacob' of the same year are both, in essence, carefully arranged studies of six male figures.

Nevertheless, 'The Surrender of Breda', painted only five years later, is an absolute triumph of complex formal composition with an appearance that is at once convincing yet cool and dispassionate. A beautiful, bluish-green light and limpid, mildly melancholy sky illuminate the scene of post-siege devastation and contrasting human chivalry. In the flesh this treasure from the Prado's permanent collection seems every bit as worthy of public awe as Rembrandt's so-called 'Night Watch' at the Rijksmuseum.

The current exhibition in Madrid exceeds even the scope of that on view last year at the Metropolitan Museum of Art in New York and takes place, moreover, in its true habitat. By the adding of extensive borrowings from major collections in other countries to the works held already in Spain, the exhibition's organisers present us with a unique and unrepeatable experience of one of the greatest and most elegant of European masters. Here is an exhibition every true art lover should endeavor to see.

Those who live in Madrid have treated the return of one of that city's more celebrated former inhabitants with extraordinary enthusiasm. During the first week of the show, visitors queued for up to five hours. Even by the time of my visit whole families were waiting in the weak February sunlight for two hours or more. The good humour of those waiting to see and later leaving the show was exemplary. Clearly astonishing art can have an extremely uplifting effect.

In my own case I went round twice in a day and came out so cheered that I could even face my more habitual viewing – of contemporary art – with good grace for some weeks to come at least.

Velazquez was not only a great observer and draughtsman but also a consummate organiser of his picture area. We observe the latter aspect not just in full-length portraits wherein even the precise pictorial proportions he chose have such a subtle bearing on the final effect. Seldom can this have been more true than in the contrasting portraits of his royal patron Philip IV and of his younger brother Don Carlos, both painted in 1626-28. The paintings are almost identical in height but the thinner proportion of that of the king serves to emphasise his height and greater gravitas.

Velazquez's human characterisations are generally more sober and also less arch somehow than those of Frans Hals although both render drapery with dazzling freedom and facility. Yet even Hals could not aspire to a portrait with the astonishing presence Velazquez gave to Juan de Pareja, his mulatto assistant.

It is tempting to imagine a great hand reached down from the sky to facilitate the making of this particular picture.

The great Prado exhibition is a triumph both of organization and orchestration. Skilled hanging makes the last great room containing

'Las Meninas', the great equestrian portraits and other superb examples a fitting climax to an overwhelming visual and spiritual experience.

I have never left an exhibition feeling more richly fed.

The Spectator UK, 17 February 1990

43

DEARTH IN VENICE

As night fell I followed three mysterious, jewel-laden women down one of the typically narrow streets which ran beside the canal.

'I need to see it and feel it before I can really get it' exclaimed one loudly to the dusky heavens. 'It's got to grab me or it's nowhere' one of her companions rejoined every bit as forthrightly, at the top of her voice. Vocal volume revealed the three to be American while their subject, disappointingly, turned out to be nothing more interesting than modern art.

Modern art was the reason the four of us were in Venice, rather than to enjoy ourselves. The Americans clearly felt their subjective feelings were sufficient in themselves to ratify what they were seeing as art. Was this the level to which art criticism had sunk at last?

All along the Grand Canal garish posters proclaimed yet another disinterring of the unengaging art of the late Andy Warhol. Amid the breathtaking architectural beauty of Venice one was confronted continually by the bland insensibility of the late Warhol's images of the equally late Marilyn Monroe.

A retrospective of Andy's catatonic work was currently filling the Palazzo Grassi.

We were reminded at every turn that once every two years modern art becomes very big business indeed for Venice. Yet in ten years' time the Italian foreign ministry intends to take the lure of the lire into another dimension altogether by bringing World Expo 2000 to this ancient, fragile watery city. Does such willingness to put an irreplaceable past at risk bear out the uncomfortable suspicion that quite a few Italian politicians would be perfectly happy to sell their grandmothers if needs arose?

By contrast with the threatened Expo the Venice Biennale brings visitors to the city at a level the existing infrastructure can just about accommodate. Hotels and restaurants were full nevertheless and each vaporetto I took or saw was crowded. The present Biennale is the 44th. Older hands than I tell me they feel disillusioned increasingly with the realities of the recent past; both dealers and artists seem to be growing more and more cynical and venal.

Jenny Holzer, the American artist whose fund of platitudes seems as inexhaustible as the dumb, inexplicable patience of her admirers, began advertising her candidature for a prize as early as Venice airport. A display board which beams her eminently forgettable flashing messages has infiltrated the other boards which provide more legitimate and useful information for incoming passengers. Out in the streets, souvenir stands carry the American prophetess's message to the multitudes in the form of tawdry hats and tee-shirts.

The Americans are reputed to have spent $2 million on their pavilion for this year's occasion. Thus Ms Holzer's comments on life have left behind their natural habitat of the cheap Christmas cracker and have become carved instead in finest marble floor tiles and benches in the American pavilion. Does this make any of her homely aphorisms, such as 'IT IS MAN's FATE TO OUTSMART HIMSELF' or 'IT IS A GIFT TO THE WORLD NOT TO HAVE BABIES' one whit less bland or complacent? Ms Holzer's wince-inducing platitudes cover more or less the entire range of remarks one hopes one will never hear at a dinner party: 'EATING TOO MUCH IS CRIMINAL', 'PRIVATE PROPERTY CREATED CRIME', 'RAISE BOYS AND GIRLS THE SAME WAY'.

Generally Holzer's woodshed wisdom strikes me as more confused than Confucian, nor is English grammar her strong point. Is Ms Holzer as grim and humourless as the average American feminist or does she contemplate her world fame each day with paroxysms of hysterical disbelief? Regrettably my own thoughts on life, art or even Ms Holzer are unlikely to find themselves carved in *rosso magnaboschi* or *nero marquina* marble floor tiles, but if they were I like to think I would have the decency to roll about on these laughing uncontrollably.

The main events of the Venice Biennale take place in the gardens which house the permanent pavilions of the 40-odd participating nations and in the appropriately named Old Rope works where the best efforts of some scores of up-and-coming artists are displayed for evaluation – if not for money. With so many exhibits to see, ample statistical evidence exists from which to adduce apparent world tendencies. Thus there is very little painting and less and less evidence of handmade marks in art of any kind. This was a source of real disappointment to me because the marks artists make are generally highly revealing of the character of the artist and of his or her mastery of the medium.

Australia chose a brace of Aboriginal painters, Switzerland a solo minimalist, Iceland an idiosyncratic painter of myth and legend, Yugoslavia one of the most meaning-free abstract expressionists I have seen so far. The German Democratic Republic offered probably the closest thing to recognisable mainstream painting in the worthy work of Walter Libuda, whose method shared something with the late Kokoschka.

Probably painting accounted for only a quarter of all the work exhibited. But did that figure provide a true reflection of any global tendency? The answer is certainly not. I suspect that most nations have worked out by now that what passes for sculpture provides an altogether safer and easier choice. Also because large sculptures fill much more of the interior spaces of national pavilions it can be seen as more imposing. Not to put too fine a point on it, the cleverer and more artistically ambitious nations are decorating their pavilions now rather than filling them with art. In some cases artists have pierced their works into or actually made holes in the fabric of their national pavilions. In the case of the French pavilion a narrow slit cut into the building's brickwork provided a most welcome reminder of God's good greenery outside.

At the same time, it admitted the joyous sound of a jazz band drumming up interest for the Australian exhibitors. The French are the only nation not to own or to have designed their own building. Was their hole therefore a protest about that, or even the start of a demolition?

From recent evidence I fear that more and more national pavilions will be filled in the future simply with amiable-looking sculptural lumps. These could be of the burnt wood variety favoured by the Japanese, the rusty iron agglomerations preferred by Israel or the cheerful chunks of sandstone sent over by Britain's Anish Kapoor. In Kapoor's 'Void Field' 16 roughly rectilinear stones of one cubic metre remain much as they were when they left the quarry except for circular holes drilled in their tops. This work, in slightly smaller form admittedly, failed to engage me when I saw it in London earlier in the year. In Venice however this and Kapoor's other work looked just about as impressive as anything I saw. I was thus not surprised that Kapoor was awarded the Prize 2000 for artists under 35 although rising 37. Nor was I astonished altogether that the USA won the prize for what amounted to the best decorated pavilion. To have spent a great deal of money and to have got nothing for it might have seemed disappointing.

Quick learners may deduce from the foregoing that the best bet for the 1992 Biennale might be a slice of Mount Everest carved with the inscription IRONY IS COWARDICE or something equally profound. By scale and scorn alone all other exhibitors would surely feel diminished.

Not surprisingly this year's Rumanian and Polish pavilions featured installations reliving distant and recent horrors. Jozef Szajna's memories of Auschwitz likewise put the whinings and posturings of various contemporary German artist into necessary perspective. If there were a wooden spoon at this year's Biennale I would award it jointly to Holland and Spain – two of the nation's most able to boast glorious artistic histories. But Venice Biennales set no store by history of course favouring only the invincible trendiness of the moment.

Indeed those who attend and take part in these events are utterly convinced, for the most part, of the unique enlightenment and importance of the age we live in.

Usually these folk are just as sure of the absolute moral rectitude of their complacent bands of moral liberalism. That the art set before us is getting visually worse and intellectually emptier is naturally not apparent to them

To sum everything up perhaps, a pro-homosexual group at the Old Rope Works calling itself Gran Fury launched a scathing attack on the Pope's 'peculiar' moral teaching.

In short, how happy it must be for every individual at the Biennale to know for sure he or she is the only one in step.

The Spectator UK, 2 June 1990

44

TOO MANY FRENCH CONNECTIONS

As the main holiday season approaches in Australia, I find my thoughts turning increasingly and somewhat perversely to France – the land where most of my holidays were formerly spent from the days of my childhood onwards.

I should admit here that part of the reason for this sudden, renewed burst of interest in France is that I recently bought myself a new and highly detailed map of that country. That was probably a mistake since such a map provides me now with a perfect excuse for nostalgic reflections.

Not long after I arrived in this country nearly twenty years ago, an Australian television station conducted a survey among other Britons who had recently settled here. Why had they done so and what did they now miss most about their former homeland?

Most of the questions and answers were fairly predictable until some bright spark – when asked what he missed most about no longer living in London – simply replied "Paris".

I could not help applauding his wit.

France lies only thirty or so kilometres from the nearest point on the English coast yet offers such a totally different experience of life that it might just as well lie at the other end of our planet.

Australia does indeed lie at the other end of our planet, of course, yet still retains a great many common features with Britain – including language. Unlike most British schoolchildren of my day, few Australians seem to learn French which probably helps make France seem especially enigmatic – or even hostile – to many Australians. I seldom sense any great natural affinity between the two nations.

Yet curiously France had a much greater influence on the shaping of Australia than most people here acknowledge.

In short, the severity of sentences passed on large numbers of early Australians owed a great deal to the fear of civil unrest and invasion engendered by the French Revolution and by the period of the subsequent, so-called Terror which created such a tempting precedent for other homicidal maniacs of the future to follow. The latter include such notable examples as Lenin, Stalin, Hitler and Pol Pot as well as all too many others for whom 'mere' human life similarly counted for little or nothing when compared with the pursuit of seriously flawed political ideologies.

What is not commonly appreciated now, in an age of declining historical knowledge. is that the revolutionary armies of Napoleon inspired greater fear in Britain in their day – and for a more protracted period – even than the threat of German invasion during the early days of the Second World War.

Britons of the early 19th century were well aware of the horrific reputations of Napoleon's revolutionary troops from the days of the latter's campaigns in Spain. In other words, the armies whose deeds prompted Francisco Goya's famous series of etchings *The Disasters of War* were not the sort of people with whom Britons were particularly keen to share their homeland. No more terrifying artistic statement on the subject of war has probably ever been made although Goya relied for the making of his apocalyptic images on nothing more complex than simple paper and line. But it does help, of course, to be a genius.

France remains, in fact, a country with so much staggering beauty inherent in its landscape, cities, towns and major buildings that it becomes easy to overlook and even to forget just how ugly various events in that country's history have been.

Foremost among such events, for me, was the absolute tragedy of the French Revolution which is still commemorated as though it were an event of great national pride rather than one associated in any way with guilt or shame. As proof of this latter assertion we need look no further than the barbaric words of France's national anthem, the Marseillaise. In my view, the seeds of France's endless flirtation with the politics of the extreme Left remain embedded in that bloodthirsty and anachronistic diatribe. What other nation on earth still sings happily today about the tainted blood of its former inhabitants 'fertilising the furrows of its land'?

That said I feel embarrassed to admit here that my own paternal ancestors were not just French but almost certainly involved in the spread of early Protestantism in France.

By the addition of just a single 'l' to Giles my name reverts rapidly, in fact, to being wholly French since Auty is simply the name of a rural village and chateau a few kilometres North East of Montauban. In the distant days of the 17th century, Montauban was the capital of the so-called Protestant Republic of Southern France and thus one of the two main centres of Huguenot resistance. The other and more famous centre in those days was La Rochelle.

Slightly to the East of Montauban and thus nearer to the former stronghold of Albi – home of famous Albigensian religious rebellion – lies the town of Cordes sur Ciel which remains my favourite hilltop town in France even though its history is actually more heretical still since, during the earlier so-called Cathar wars of the 13th century the entire town found itself excommunicated. The French writer Albert Camus once said tellingly of Cordes: "Everything is beautiful there, even regret".

However, in spite of the Protestant pasts of my ancestors I personally became a Catholic in 1962, an event I celebrated by a first visit to Lourdes which lies in another of my favourite areas of France, not far from the Spanish frontier.

Services were still held in those pre-Vatican II days in Latin and the particular advantage of a universal language was forcibly brought home to me when I found myself singing the creed in the company of believers from all over the world. While taking part, one evening, in the famous torchlight procession I found myself flanked by fellow pilgrims from central Africa, South America and Canada. No-one around me seemed to experience any apparent problem with a language which, like many English schoolboys of my day, I first began learning – along with French and Greek – at the age of about ten.

The following day when first visiting the famous grotto at Lourdes, I experienced a sudden, overwhelming sensation of divine presence and peace which was unlike anything I had ever known. Disbelievers dismiss the cause of such experiences as 'auto-suggestion' yet I had not the slightest inkling of what was about to occur. How then could I possibly have induced it myself?

Regrettably I was not destined to visit Lourdes again until 1973 when I did so during a lengthy journey I made by car at the beginning of autumn.

Earlier in that journey, when driving through Northern Paris, I had been extremely puzzled to see scores of inhabitants out on the streets listening intently to portable radios.

The cause turned out to be the start of the so-called Yom Kippur war of that year in which Arab states – notably Syria and Egypt – prospered initially. Yet by the time I began my return journey to Britain a fortnight later Israel had totally reversed the earlier military situation and petrol prices had doubled already as a direct result of the conflict.

While finally making my way to Lourdes, I stopped briefly at the ancient walled city of Carcassonne where I sat for a while on the ramparts. Carcassonne was occupied by the Romans as early as the second century BC yet the thought came to me then that the historic France which I had known and loved since childhood would henceforward slip slowly away, unable to cope with the crueller realities of a changing world.

A few days later I crossed the channel to Dover where somewhat over-zealous customs officials made a pretty good job of taking my entire car to pieces.

For some extraordinary reason they had convinced themselves that I was carrying drugs for why else would someone drive an anonymous-looking car to the Cote d'Azur way outside the normal holiday season and then make a huge detour on the way home?

Some two years earlier an American film called *The French Connection* had dealt with an attempt by criminals from the South of France to import large quantities of heroin into America by car.

However, the rather odd truth remained that I had been commissioned to direct the photography of a book about early motor yachts many of which were still to be found around the Southern shores of France. The vast detour I had made was simply to re-visit Lourdes.

But who, given the somewhat volatile nature of the world at that precise moment, would ever have believed such a far-fetched seeming tale?

Dover's customs officers were totally convinced for some hours, at least, that they had got their man. Perhaps, as a result of my plight, they should simply have been discouraged in the future from watching high-powered American thrillers.

Annals, November 2014

45

LAMENT FOR A LAST, LOST, SEMI-INNOCENT WORLD

I paid my first visit to St. Ives in Cornwall in the late 1950s and will never forget my first glimpse of the town from the hill above the railway station.

For someone to whom the word 'sea' had hitherto largely meant the pebbly beaches and endless mudflats of the coast of East Kent, the turquoise water, dazzling white sands and rows of granite or whitewashed buildings cascading down steep hills toward the town's harbour were an utter revelation.

Not a single yard of dual carriageway existed at that time between London and Land's End. The old A.30 still ran through every town, village and hamlet on its route as it pursued its narrow, twisting and hazardous 450 kilometre course.

At least part of the magic of West Cornwall lay at the time in its relative isolation as well as in the extreme cheapness of property there which attracted painters, potters and poets – to say nothing of sculptors and assorted scribes – of national and international as well as purely local substance to its welcoming embrace.

Because an artist cousin of mine, John Peace, lived in the town already I enjoyed instant introductions to many of the area's resident talents.

During the last two months of the 1950s I returned to St. Ives with the aim of living and painting there full-time myself – an arrival which coincided closely with a highly unlikely sojourn there by Francis Bacon who basically detested rural living – and I was then resident in that general area, on and off, for the next twenty years.

What I propose here is that those two decades – from 1960 to 1980 – formed the last era which may ever exist in which some degree of communal sense, integrity and idealism will ever prevail again in British art which now, by contrast, generally seems to grow more cynical, corrupt and purposeless by the day.

To my mind, at least, one of the factors that underwrote the significance of that era was its relative proximity to the ending of the Second World War which, in spite of all its horrors, at least provided some inkling of a reality with which its was difficult to argue.

Some of the older artists such as Peter Lanyon had served in that war with a degree of distinction while others had suffered years of captivity e.g. Terry Frost, Adrian Heath and Roger Hilton who were all captured during an unsuccessful commando raid on St.Nazaire. Karl Weschke, by contrast, spent his youthful years as a prisoner-of-war of the British.

It was therefore not just artistic freedom that all were keen to enjoy after years of restraint but the liberty to live and act more or less normally again. Hedonism was certainly in the air and West Cornwall became, however briefly, a kind of Bohemia-by-Sea.

Ben Nicholson had recently left St. Ives for good at the time of my arrival there but others such as Bryan Wynter, Patrick Heron, Barbara Hepworth, Bernard Leach and the excellent Scottish poet W.S.Graham were still very much in evidence as were Alan Davie and William Scott for at least part of the time. I was merely one of a great raft of younger artists which included Trevor Bell, Anthony Benjamin, Brian Wall, Bob Law, Jeff Harris and Roy Conn. Large numbers of purpose-built studios still existed from earlier eras and for a time I was lucky enough to share a vast example, built originally for the Newlyn School painter Stanhope Forbes, at the top of Newlyn Hill.

In the long run I came to disagree increasingly with the tenor of much of the art – and art criticism – that came out of West Cornwall at that time because its doctrinaire emphasis on abstraction seemed to me at once unnecessarily coercive and contrived in the face of the overwhelming majesty of the local landscape and coast.

My maternal great-grandfather, who was a railway engineer, originally left his birthplace at East Looe in Cornwall to build a railway in Kent and I have never ceased, wherever I have since lived in the world, to feel a kind of ancestral tug which continues to identify Cornwall for me as a homeland.

Rather unusually, for an artist, I represented the county at cricket and am still probably remembered there, if at all, more for my former prowess with a cricket ball than with a paintbrush.

All of the artists I have mentioned already were certainly ambitious but not in the degrading way which, in more recent times, has almost become a norm.

It was at the Royal College of Art in 1962, I think, that I first heard the ominous expression 'making it' used in connection with David Hockney to whom I had just been introduced.

To artists such as the late Roger Hilton or Peter Lanyon such an expression would rightly have been anathema. What precisely was the 'it' the artist was supposed to be 'making'?

Money and largely unearned fashionable fame? Or a reputation blown up simply with a giant public relations bicycle pump?

During the last two and a half years of his life Roger Hilton, who was confined to bed with a painful illness, produced a series of small, colourful gouaches of unending wit and good humour.

Roger had a very sharp tongue indeed, however, and it would have been intriguing and instructive to have known what he might have thought of future events such as the Turner Prize which have consistently divided the world of British art since his death.

Both he and the amiable and elegant painter Bryan Wynter died within a fortnight of each other in 1975. After attending Bryan's funeral, in fact, at the lovely little rural church at Zennor a small group of us travelled on to visit Roger.

I was seated at the end of the latter's bed still clad in the black overcoat I had worn to Bryan's funeral when Roger suddenly cried out to me – rather prophetically, in the event – "you are the Angel of Death come to carry me away".

Roger had always possessed a strange, almost psychic awareness.

Read, if you possibly can, the two deeply moving and remarkably beautiful poems which W.S.Graham wrote as a tribute to his departed friends: *Dear Bryan Wynter* and *Lines on Roger Hilton's Watch*.

Both feature in *W.S. Graham Collected Poems 1942-1977* (Faber & Faber 1979) and both capture something of the departed magic of West Cornwall as an artists' colony with an eloquence I cannot hope to match.

Who remembers figures such as Hilton and W.S.Graham today less than 40 years after their passing? Both were true to their respective callings as painter and poet in ways we have become less and less likely ever to encounter again.

During the last years of West Cornwall's artistic heyday the trio of Hilton, Graham and Wynter drank regularly at a large, isolated and often almost deserted pub situated on the coast road from Zennor to St.Just. This was The Gurnard's Head whose landlord bought the lease, I believe, with the gratuity he received as an officer when leaving the Parachute Regiment.

On nights of heavy rain or fog when the pub was almost deserted 'Jock' Graham would write and direct, off-the-cuff one-act plays for those privileged to be present. Very occasionally a lost visitor would stumble out of the inclement weather outside into one of these proceedings.

"There came a mighty wind" Graham shouted on one occasion as he leapt out of a dark corner just as a lost visitor staggered in.

As a landlord, Jimmy Goodman's particular *betes noires* were men who drove Jaguars or who were connected in any way with advertising, the making of television commercials or films.

Alone among those living in the area therefore he refused to acknowledge the fact when the film *Straw Dogs* was being shot just down the road at the village of St.Buryan.

One evening however the strikingly pretty actress Susan George, who was featuring in the film, apparently burst into Jimmy's pub saying "I'm Susan George and I'm looking for my co-star Dustin Hoffman".

Jimmy pondered her request slowly before finally replying thus: "I've been the landlord here for many years m'dear and can assure you there are no coastguards of that name working in this area".

Clearly, given the way the modern world has subsequently developed, such times were too wonderful to last.

The Jackdaw UK, January/February 2014

46

MAGICAL MEMORIES OF PLACE AND TIME

In the past few days a valued friend – the widely admired Australian painter John Olsen – sent me an unexpected but utterly delightful gift: a handmade, limited-edition book about the life and work of a Cornish artist I once knew, the late Peter Lanyon 1918-1964.

This lengthy and beautiful book, which is full of artistic insights plus comments actually uttered by the artist, was prepared as a tribute – with help from other members of the family – by one of that artist's sons.

However accurate our own memories may be of periods from our earlier lives, it remains amazing nevertheless how the biographical recollections of other people we once knew can re-animate the past for us. Indeed, simply by dipping into this book I shortly found myself transported back to my own first spell in Cornwall which lasted from 1959 until not long after the time of Peter's untimely death in 1964 in a crash involving the glider he was flying.

Although seated as I write in my study in the Blue Mountains of NSW I can almost taste once more the salt tang of the Atlantic which regularly hits the granite shores of West Cornwall with a force built up slowly over thousands of kilometres of unbroken ocean.

Lanyon was an out-and-out Cornishman although – rather unusually as such – he was sent away to be educated in another county. The whole, magical ambience of far West Cornwall, created in part by its wealth of ancient menhirs (standing stones), pre-Christian hill forts, stone circles and lanyons (ancient burial chambers covered by vast flat rocks), affected him personally and very deeply.

I, by contrast, enjoy much more distant Cornish ancestry solely because my mother's paternal grandfather, who was a railway engineer, once travelled from the small Cornish town of East Looe to the county of Kent to help build one of Britain's earlier railways. Hence my own maternal grandfather and all of his children were born in the latter county.

That said, West Cornwall has probably been the area in my own life – out of an ample range of contrasting national and international locations – where I have thus far felt most at home.

However, what this new addition to my library has awoken in me – even more perhaps than a nostalgia for place – is a heady consciousness of times past.

Such consciousness now prompts me to wonder, for example, how we have passed in little more than fifty years from those distant, largely innocent and optimistic days of 1964 to our present nervous, pessimistic and sometimes apocalyptic-seeming times.

Does anyone imagine even for a moment that such changes happen by accident?

If not, then what is your personal theory about why the Western world has seemingly changed so fast and in some ways, at least, so disagreeably?

1964, which was the year of Lanyon's death, also witnessed what was then a little remarked on birth – that of the notion of so-called political correctness at a Californian university.

Yet do you now know even a single adult to whom the term 'politically correct' is unfamiliar?

Basically, political correctness is an attempted form of thought control through which demands for ideological conformity encroach on the traditional foundations of our intellectual and social freedoms.

So why on earth did we allow such an insidious form of alien totalitarianism to enter our democratic bloodstream in Australia?

Were we all half asleep?

Political correctness has, of course, been just one of the various forms of attempted social coercion which have tried to transform Western society from something broadly based on traditional Christian precepts to a form of society ruled largely now by some novel, godless and entirely man-made notion of morality.

Is there any wonder that we sometimes feel so lost or floundering?

When Peter Lanyon effectively set forth on his professional artistic journey in 1945, following distinguished service with the RAF in the Second World War, the basic struggles he faced were simply to develop his undoubted talent for art and somehow to feed a growing family.

What a wonderfully straightforward world all of that now seems.

Television barely existed then, let alone the complex and often frightening implications of the internet or of our so-called social media. Banks even existed then which aimed to fulfil their time-honoured social functions rather than attempting singlehandedly to destroy the entire economy of our planet. Best of all for me perhaps patronage of the visual arts was still confined almost entirely to choices made by private purchasers. The long reign of wasteful and opinionated arts councils and such had by then still barely begun.

If he were still alive, Peter Lanyon would by now be in his late nineties.

I knew him at least fairly well as a man of passionate enthusiasms who soaked up experiences of all kinds which he later attempted to recycle visually as the essence of his art.

Lanyon's best paintings, in my view, were thus a kind of eclectic synthesis of deeply felt personal experiences

When I first lived in West Cornwall myself I often made long, solitary walks such as along the famous section of coastal footpath which runs all the way – about 65 kms – from St. Ives to Penzance. The path was heavily overgrown in those days – because very little used – and while walking on a remote section of it one day I was therefore amazed to see a group of people swimming far below me in a cove I had always believed to be completely inaccessible. Clambering down some very difficult terrain, however, I came eventually on a group of seals which were playing together in the water as happily as any set of their human counterparts could conceivably do.

Did you know that if you sing loudly enough on deserted Cornish beaches at night seals will often come to you however inadequate your choral charms? Is that also the case with seals in Australia? I imagine it probably must be.

In days gone by the naturally clannish indigenous Cornish referred to all non-local holidaymakers as 'emmets' – the local word for ants – even though the county relied heavily on the revenue such visitors once provided.

Tourism apart, that remote county's other main sources of income were formerly the production of kaolin – or china clay – plus inshore and deep-sea fishing. The latter industry has, however, largely collapsed by now owing to the depredations of huge foreign trawlers which are insufficiently controlled by European Union regulations.

Lanyon was a maker of spontaneous-looking, semi-abstract productions which nevertheless always retained recognisable physical elements such as a fast-moving fox racing across a distant hillside. His was an intensely human art, in fact, which combined personal memory with a consciousness of longer-term history, often of a specifically local and idiosyncratic nature. Whatever the outcome of his art one was always aware of the pleasure – as well as intense effort – of its making.

The joy of making was once considered one of the birthrights of the true artist – yet how many works created today look as they would give even the slightest pleasure to construct?

Since Lanyon's death more than fifty years ago we have witnessed the increasing degeneration of almost every known art form as it has become either increasingly commercialised, politicised or subject to some gross form of populism.

Society as a whole has clearly been the loser.

The book John Olsen gave me reminds me however of a time when the intrinsic merits of paintings, poetry, novels, plays and films were still very widely and passionately debated as a regular feature of normal human discourse.

Where did our passion go for genuine, original and deeply moving art rather than just for generally banal 'blockbusters' or 'box-office' successes?

Art which truly survives involves the world of the spirit which was still such a vital and widely acknowledged aspect of normal human life even a half century ago.

As an isolated country which is often uncertain of itself Australia can especially ill afford the loss here of any unifying spiritual dimension.

It is very hard at times not to see much of the progress we claim in almost every sector of our lives as being, in reality, just sadly and quite pathetically regressive.

Annals, April/May 2015

47

LEARNING CURVES

In the last issue of *Annals* I touched on the vital importance of culture in its broadest sense to our everyday lives and in the issue before that wrote about the important ways in which our physical surroundings affect us.

Australia has many facets and achievements of which we can be justly proud but I do not think that the variety or outright quality of our cultural life is necessarily one of those although I may obviously make myself unpopular by saying so.

I basically came here to live and work twenty years ago and look back at least occasionally now in a state of amusement and considerable disbelief at some of my earliest experiences of this country.

Thus on an initial visit to Darwin to cover the annual Aboriginal art awards there I was approached politely after the show by a group of important local citizens who chose, most surprisingly, to throw a dinner party in my honour.

I should emphasise here that the reason they had done so probably had rather less to do with me than the fact that for many years before coming here I had been a columnist for what was then a wholly British publication: *The Spectator.*

Indeed it was their degree of weekly reliance on the wit, sophistication, originality and political wisdom of that magazine that formed the vital bond which held my various distinguished hosts together. As one of the latter admitted to me later on: "You simply can't imagine what a welcome degree of style, culture and civilization a foreign magazine like *The Spectator* brings to those of us who live in such an isolated outpost as Darwin. For my part, at least, it may even have helped keep me sane".

When the dinner party finally broke up one of my hosts kindly offered me a lift back to my hotel.

First, though, he asked me to help remove a stick insect of about the length and girth of a car jack from the windscreen of his vehicle where it was clinging with great determination to the wiper blades.

Had I ever encountered such insects before?

I assured him that I had but remarked that the largest I had seen previously – in a pet shop in London – would certainly have been no more than a few centimetres long.

It was at that precise point that I began to realise just how much I had yet to learn about the physical parameters and topography of Australia.

It was not long after that, in fact, that I also realized just how much I had to learn about the psychological parameters of life here too when a review I had written about an Australian book for the pages of *The Spectator* caused me to be hauled before the editor-in-chief of the Australian paper which then employed me.

What kind of hideous solecism had I innocently committed?

The precise nature of my offence had been to describe the nature of intellectual life in Australia in my review as "rather less than effervescent".

Indeed the nature of the entirely humourless reaction of an editor of one of our major newspapers might have seemed to provide plenty of evidence to confirm my view.

No less absurdly my supposed solecism was quoted subsequently in a book about another former art critic for *The Australian*. Indeed my casual, off-the-cuff remark was then held to provide conclusive proof of my lack of suitablity to work in such a sophisticated country as this.

Thankfully Australia has grown up substantially since those less than edifying days and *The Spectator* has also been published for some years now in an Australian edition which upholds many of the fine qualities of the original.

However, outside *Annals* which has been kind enough to publish me now for many years the outlets for genuinely thoughtful writing still seem to me to remain fairly thin on the ground in Australia – at least for those of us who are not of a particularly entrenched Left-wing political mindset.

Politically correct, anti-religious Left wing bias extends also – with certain honourable exceptions – to much of the world of Australian publishing and I draw your attention once again here to the perceptive words of John O'Sullivan in last month's *Quadrant* which I quoted from quite extensively in my last piece for *Annals*.

Other than our own editor's recent, yet to be concluded but epic series on the history of Islam – which demands much wider recognition – O'Sullivan's comments on the current shortcomings of Australian culture provide a sharp analysis of where we are exactly and where we should aspire to be. For Australian intellectual life is not just – as I remarked nearly twenty years ago – "rather less than effervescent" but by now is also all too frequently parochial, myopic and even downright lazy.

In short, the generally lacklustre nature of a large part of our home-grown 'culture' is a poor reflection by now on a nation which wishes to be thought of as civilized. Indeed, in spite of my strong revulsion for Islamic acts of terrorism I could not avoid feeling some slight sympathy for the assertion of a recently arrested Muslim youth that much of our present way of life here is decidedly decadent.

I was a small child during the Second World War and grew up in an era of general privation and of fairly tough personal choices for most people. That said, in the English country area where my parents lived the strength of community spirit, neighbourliness and mutual respect nevertheless puts large tracts of our present-day world to shame.

At one time Australia was by repute a highly hospitable and community-conscious nation but I have strong doubts whether we are still quite as friendly to outsiders or even to ourselves as we once claimed to be.

Nearly half a century ago now a concerted attempt was made – by spoilt university students among others – in a number of Western countries to try to overthrow as many existing cultural, social and religious traditions as possible and to supplant these with what I personally regard as an entirely ersatz culture which is frequently founded on little more than rhetorical propaganda and the mouthing of empty slogans. In few areas has this generally mindless campaign been more successful – sadly for me – than in the visual arts.

Often the novel rhetoric on offer simply proved self-fulfilling as in the supposed existence of 'a permissive society' and where it was not – as in the case of so-called political correctness, for example – social and legal coercion were soon called in to lend a helping hand.

Truth of any kind became merely one of the early victims of the new modes of thinking and in what seemed no time at all the word truth itself became a synonym in the minds of the ignorant simply for personal opinion.

One after another the novel platitudes were trotted out and shortly most became lodged immovably in the minds of those many whose education had become increasingly politicized as well as dumbed down.

Wonderful new words were invented to describe what were certainly meant to be refreshing new initiatives.

So-called multiculturalism is just one obvious case in point.

The word sounds brimming with virtue but what does it truly signify to the average Australian?

A slightly larger choice of local 'foreign' restaurants perhaps?

Probably the most important issue in terms of future social cohesion is that all would-be immigrants should basically subscribe to the culture, laws and vital traditions of their host country – and should also make a solemn, legally enforceable vow to do so.

Following the Second World War many thousands of immigrants undertook to do more or less precisely that when coming to Australia – a valuable process which also led in time to an enviable degree of integration.

It should be obvious here that skin colour is infinitely less important in such a context than any would-be immigrant's core beliefs but somehow the two unrelated issues soon became muddled in the minds of many.

A true post-modernist probably regards all forms of religious belief as anachronistic forms of superstition and may well hope that all who think otherwise may shortly be converted to his or her more sophisticated views. Herein lies one of the principal weaknesses of so-called multiculturalism. In short it is often promoted and advocated by those who are utterly incapable of understanding its most crucial – that is religious issues – themselves.

The word ghetto once referred exclusively to Jewish areas within a city but today encompasses areas of ethnic and religious diversity of a great many kinds not just in Australia but in great swathes of our world. The existence of ghettos, *per se,* thus undermines the basic dream of the multiculturalist because what immigrants most often try to replicate as closely as possible is the condition of living in their own former or traditional lands.

In a huge number of cases, in fact, they are simply economic migrants rather than those genuinely fleeing oppression.

I am grateful to have become an Australian citizen myself but frequently feel frustrated by the lack of opportunities I have received to contribute much more actively to the life of this nation.

The probable reason for that is that I am thought to hold too many 'wrong views' even though many of the latter are surely shared by a great many of those who would like to help re-establish some kind of proper backbone for this country.

I fear the entirely valid dream of an 'old' Australia – which first attracted me here – is slowly but surely vanishing before our eyes.

Annals, November 2015

48

HAS ANTI-CATHOLICISM RETURNED?

Not long after Tony Abbott's thoughtful and well-argued book *Battlelines* was published by Melbourne University Press in 2009 I wrote a piece for this publication called *The Next Catholic in Kirribilli*.

Mr. Abbott was not even leader of his own party at the time so I feel that I – along with *Annals* – can claim some degree of prescience at least in this matter.

Some six years later Mr.Abbott has indeed come and in my view surprisingly gone from Kirribilli as well as from this country's top political job.

Last week I attended a dinner organized by the monthly magazine *Quadrant* in Sydney at which Gerald Henderson and Greg Sheridan discussed their recently published books on B.A. Santamaria and Abbott and Sheridan's youthful lives respectively.

I met B.A.Santamaria only once at a dinner held at the Celtic Club in Melbourne that was organized to raise funds for the making and erection of a bronze of the late Archbishop Mannix for the grounds of St.Patrick's Cathedral – a work I personally commissioned on behalf of then Archbishop Pell. To my great surprise B.A. Santamaria knew my writings well as did George Pell who had been reading me for years apparently in the pages of the then wholly British weekly *The Spectator*. In the case of the latter, at least, such knowledge of my views had encouraged him to seek my advice on matters in which I luckily had some specialist knowledge.

I had not attended a *Quadrant* dinner for some time until last week because until last year I lived for some while in England.

Such occasions represent a meeting place largely for traditional Liberal voters, a good proportion of whom – based on my own observations – seemed to be Catholics. I was especially interested to learn from the latter that many believe a large part of this country's opposition to Mr.Abbott stemmed from the latter's Catholicism *in itself*.

Politics are particularly prey to rhetorical use of language whereby even the most unsafe and untested political initiatives – such as gay marriage for instance – become described inevitably as 'progress' and 'progressive' more or less throughout our media.

Anyone who has reservations about such ideas thus soon finds himself described as being 'against progress' of course.

By now that must surely be the oldest and hoariest political trick in the book?

Unfortunately with the sad intellectual ineptitude apparent in so many of our voters – which is an inevitable consequence in itself of compulsory voting – even the simplest of rhetorical tricks and slogans remain hugely effective still in this country.

Compulsory voting remains an insuperable barrier in fact to this nation's admirable urge to grow up.

In my view compulsory voting is essentially anti-democratic in nature and thus militates against the forming of any proper democracy here. That is possibly the last thing we need.

Happily, through coming from overseas, the recently appointed editor of *Quadrant* brings a fresh pair of eyes to the affairs of this country and I therefore salute the following words extracted from John O'Sullivan's most recent editorial in that magazine as providing the most constructive suggestions I have read so far on the future of conservatism in Australia, whether Catholic or otherwise. John O'Sullivan who is an Irish-born Catholic himself was previously an adviser to the conservative government in Britain:

> There is a safer and better way to advance the broad
> conservative interest now hostage to Liberal Party

decisions. That is to devote more energy and thought to making the conservative movement directly influential in Australian life and culture. Liberal timidity and Malcolm Turnbull's ambitions are far less of an obstacle to conservative ideas and values than the stranglehold the Left has on cultural institutions from universities to publishing to the theatre to television sitcoms to news and current affairs to legal training. Instead of encouraging able young conservatives to sink into the political class, we should be directing them into film schools, art galleries, law journals, publishing houses, charities, foundations, orchestras, newsrooms, magazine start-ups, and all the occupations that shape and elevate our minds and imaginations. Once there is an active and conservative cultural environment, then *both* political parties will find that their policy choices have somehow been pushed in a conservative direction (or at least not pushed in a liberal direction) without anyone quite knowing why or how. For that to happen, however, we need bold cultural leadership by prominent people.

During the otherwise creditable Prime Ministership of John Howard cultural issues were broadly ignored and neglected. These were not his areas of particular interest or expertise admittedly but all of society pays a price when the importance of culture in the broadest sense is neglected. Why does the ABC, for example, still pursue an attitude of perennial hostility to the Catholic Church?

Santamaria and others fought an epic battle to save Australia from communism at the time of the Cold War. I have had experience few Australians have shared of travelling and working in former communist countries when the regimes there were still in full cry. I also did military service when war with Russia was a distinct possibility.

The Western world is in turmoil at present and is in need of moral leadership as never before. Yet the media plays a major role in Australia in contributing to the fragility and nervousness of our political life.

When will a leader emerge again here who understands the vital importance of decency, loyalty and a consistent moral code in international as well as national affairs?

Unfortunately I find myself unable to answer my own question.

Annals, October 2015

49

WHAT DID YOU DO IN THE CULTURE WARS DADDY?

As I look round this distinguished gathering I recognise very few faces so presume this lack of recognition may be mutual.

That was not always the case. Until about 10 years ago I visited Melbourne regularly while I was still working for *The Australian.*

Indeed in those days I enjoyed a particular distinction in this city. Apparently, if conversation ever flagged at polite Melbourne dinner parties, mere mention of my name was enough to set everyone at each other's throats.

I have always believed that criticism of any kind should evoke at least some sort of response so suppose I ought to feel pleased.

Unfortunately for me, for some years now, a general impression seems to have existed in Australia that I am either dead or that I moved back some time ago to the United Kingdom.

However, since I appear to be standing here and about to address you, I hope you will agree that while such views about me may be prescient they are not entirely accurate.

The person you see is not therefore a ghost but simply an example of an international cultural commentator who has found himself marginalised fairly effectively in this country.

I admit that is not a condition I especially enjoy.

I thus join a list of Britons and other Europeans engaged in the arts who have learned this kind of lesson the hard way.

If you think here of the fairly recent history of the Australian Ballet, Opera Australia or the National Gallery of Australia I sense you will grasp what I mean.

What madness possessed any of us outsiders to believe we could succeed here within an entrenched and largely parochial left-wing culture which generally seems content with very undemanding standards indeed yet claims these nonetheless to be among the world's best?

I was planning to talk today largely about what I perceive as the failure of most public arts patronage in Australia but have just read a cogent article by Michael Connor in the June edition of *Quadrant* which makes much of what I had to say on that subject seem superfluous.

Connor's article sets the problem out with great clarity and also endorses my own findings more or less exactly. However, unlike me, there can be no accusation that Connor is a being critical as an outsider since so far as I know he was born here.

Because Connor's article is hostile to the existing status quo in the arts in Australia the number of publications which would be willing even to consider publishing it is pathetically small: the *IPA Review* would, of course, be one and obviously *Quadrant* but outside these two the outlets are probably limited to the few pages of Australian content in the Australian edition of *The Spectator.* Clearly the Fairfax press would not touch an article such as Connor's with a bargepole nor would the ABC which possibly leaves not much more than the arts or literary pages of *The Australian.* However, on recent evidence, including my own, a contribution such as Connor's would not necessarily be especially welcome there either.

Here is a short excerpt from Connor's article: "The intense Howard-hatred we lived through from 1996 to 2007 will not just be repeated if an Abbott government is elected – it will be far worse. The Left's slide into barbarism is not hidden in obscure corners of the web but is a daily product of ABC commentary pages, the Fairfax press, and much-visited Left blogs. Culture will again be a battleground, and the Coalition's lack of reformist policy for dealing with the arts will ensure that they will again go into battle against enemies they themselves have funded".

The neo-Marxist, post-modernist faithful who over forty years ago proposed A Long March through the enfeebled cultural and educational institutions of the West have possibly succeeded beyond even their wildest dreams in Australia.

Michael Connor's article in the current edition of *Quadrant* is aptly called *Arts Policy and the Culture of Grovel.*

It throws light on just about every area of inept bureaucratic ideology that I first began to highlight and attack myself in the area of public patronage of the arts in Britain over forty years ago.

Here's how Connor sums the whole thing up: "Government patronage of the arts produces politicised bureaucrats not artists. Good intentions have produced a politicised Left culture of grovel, elitism and stupidity. If the Coalition is ever to do anything to free us from this it needs analysis, discussion, policy planning, and the will to introduce change. The 'culture wars' highlighted a deep dissatisfaction with cultural institutions perverted by the Left, a dissatisfaction felt by the broad community, who show an instinctive distrust of our cultural malaise, but did not present policy for dealing with the problems. Until they are confronted and adopted by the Coalition, we are condemning future generations to the same fate of bureaucratic cultural misery which is promoted as Australia's cultural glory by those who live off it."

The foregoing are pretty strong words.

But I should stress here that Australia's and the Australia Council's problems are certainly not unique. In England I fought, in the company of notable others, an uphill battle with the Arts Council of Great Britain and its subsidiaries over many years. I also served on an Advisory Committee for the Arts and Heritage for the conservative government of the day and fought a similarly uphill fight as a member of The Art Working Group for the National Curriculum for English and Welsh Schools. My appointment to the latter committee was almost certainly the work of Margaret Thatcher who had no illusions at all about the pervasive left-wing bias at the time of Britain's system of public education.

Contrary to today's received wisdom on the subject, public patronage has been the least successful by far of the four forms of patronage known so far to the West. Perhaps we should all take a look here at what patronage by the pre-Reformation Catholic Church, patronage by royalty and nobility and patronage by a burgeoning bourgeoisie and great commercial patrons actually produced in an historical context?

Such latter forms of patronage were, of course, a major and integral part of The Genius of Western Civilisation. There is scarcely an artist of unquestioned historical status who was not a product of such patronage. Indeed the Medicis alone probably achieved more through their inspired patronage than all the present, publicly- funded patronage which will ever exist.

For me, a vital component of The Genius of Western Civilisation has also been the regular existence among older nations, at least, of what I see as a self-righting mechanism.

Unfortunately, unlike older-established nations, Australia lacks any such self-righting mechanism almost entirely. I speak here of a mechanism which operates, on the whole, through timely recourse to the wisdom of major traditions – not the least of which is simple commonsense – and to other 'calls to order' all of which can help to right the listing cultural or political ship.

The relative youth of the Australian nation is also one of the reasons why second-rate and occasionally malignant ideas take root and flourish here so readily. I think here especially not just of communist ideology itself but also of a raft of the often pernicious orthodoxies – such as relativism and political correctness – which together constitute post-modernism. As we all should realise by now, a high percentage of such orthodoxies are themselves neo-Marxist in origin.

Without some colossal re-energising of the national psyche I fear the battle against such orthodoxies will be effectively lost in Australia and that this country may never emerge again from beneath their yoke.

In Australia, secularised Christianity once provided a bulwark and some kind of desirable social cement for this country's moral spine. Unfortunately that backbone is under consistent and conscious daily assault itself now from post-modernism's more militant proponents in the Australian media.

I do not wish to base my comments on the current state of Australian culture and public patronage too much merely on my own experience which is one reason why I have quoted extensively from Michael Connor.

On the other hand some brief record of my personal experience may also be thought to provide clear evidence of worrying political bias in Australian culture.

I was appointed as national arts correspondent by the then editor in chief of *The Australian* Paul Kelly during a lecture tour I made here in 1994.

However, before my feet had done much more than touch the tarmac at Sydney airport to take up that role in May 1995 an article of extreme hostility 'about' me appeared in *The Age*. This was compiled entirely from hostile comments from known opponents of mine in Britain and of hostile opinions from Australians I had yet to meet. Why, for example, did those who compiled that article not contact my former editors at *The Spectator*? At *The Australian* itself Elwyn Lynn refused to work with me in spite of an amicable offer from me to share duties while a further art critic employed by that paper merely refused to speak to me. That made our joint operations for the paper somewhat difficult to arrange. Not long after that I was approached by the ABC who wished to make a program about me. In the course of so doing they interviewed me for five hours and then boiled my contribution down to just five minutes complete with some utterly vile and grossly dishonest editing. The rest of the program was further padded out by contributions from further apparent enemies I had yet to meet in the Australian media. I wonder where this particularly disgraceful piece of TV making is today? Perhaps we should all be privileged with a re-run as yet further proof of the gross and long-established political bias of the ABC?

From my own experience and clearly that of other Europeans it appears that reputations gained elsewhere count for little or nothing in a predominantly blinkered, biased and leftist culture here.

I believe this to be a profound pity for without such outside contributions a largely parochial culture such as Australia's can all too easily simply stagnate.

I came to Australia in a spirit of great optimism and goodwill and would like to have made some more lasting contributions to the cultural life of this country.

For example, looking straight in front of me as I speak I see His Eminence Cardinal Pell.

When he was merely Catholic Archbishop of Melbourne, His Eminence approached me to advise him on commissioning a large bronze of Archbishop Mannix and other improvements for the precincts of St.Patrick's Cathedral and the cathedral itself.

I gave him the best advice I could and he was kind enough to act on it. I hope you will agree that what we did between us has turned out to be a significant success.

For me, my great frustration is that my abilities and knowledge have not been employed more often during my time here in Australia since I certainly came here with the highest of hopes.

Before coming to Australia I had never even heard of the expression 'tall poppy syndrome' but can confirm for all those in doubt about its very existence that the famous phenomenon is still very much alive and well.

Sadly it provides an indelible stain on the life of a country of which we could all otherwise be justifiably proud.

Institute of Public Affairs, address given at the Western Civilization
Conference, Melbourne 2012

50

BRITAIN'S SOCIAL DIVIDE: DIALECT OR DIALECTIC?

Although I have lived in Australia on and off for about 15 years I admit to being woefully inept at identifying this nation's regional accents even if they can still genuinely be held to exist. Queenslanders apart, who interject 'eh' every three to four words, I haven't a clue whether a speaker hails from Blayney or Burnie.

In Britain, by contrast, I would back myself to identify any fellow Pom's place of origin pretty accurately partly because a number of very common words give the game away.

Foremost among these is the numeral 'one' which is pronounced variously as 'won' or 'wan' – as in want. Here is a highly reliable indicator as to whether the speaker comes from South or North of a line drawn just below Britain's midlands. The word 'bath' is another useful guide which similarly divides the country. Those saying bath as in 'path' come from South of the line while those preferring baths as in 'maths' come from comfortably above it.

It was to the great chagrin of the wife of a friend that her husband could not even pronounce the name 'properly' of the historic city in which they lived: Bath.

Just down the road from Bath lies the city of Bristol – a name modified by many of its inhabitants to 'bristle'. To true locals Britain's second city is similarly 'burbigum' while outside the walls of the city, at least, many still refer to this as Birmingham.

How, on the other hand, might one identify an authentic inhabitant of Britain's Newcastle without risk of error? The standard test proposed to me once was to persuade the person in question to read the following phrase: "eighty eight bacon and egg sandwiches' – from which the last three words are superfluous.

For the moment you hear "yatety yate beeyaken" you know your respondent is a genuine Geordie. The latter also pronounce 'boat' as a two syllable word.

Sometimes, however, it is the choice of word rather than the manner of its rendering which provides the vital clue.

In Edinburgh, for instance, bitterly cold mornings are widely described as 'fraysh' (fresh) while in East Yorkshire similarly icy mornings are often known as 'thin' or 'narrer' (narrow).

When not living in London, two of the English counties in which I spent quite a lot of time were Devon and Cornwall – both of which boast strong regional accents.

However, these and the adjoining county of Somerset present great problems for aspiring actors of both sexes who learn at stage school to speak a concocted Westcountry tongue which has never genuinely been spoken anywhere. Outside the profession, at least, this is generally and sometimes contemptuously referred to as "mummerset'. "Thank you koind zur" is an example of the above. Mummers were, of course, all-male bands of strolling actors and minstrels who entertained their fellow countrymen half a millennium ago.

Genuine Devonian and Cornish accents are harder to imitate than many suppose and often it is choice of local words or strange constructions which confer authenticity.

Thus in Devon the verb to 'urge' (vomit) is one I have never encountered elsewhere yet was once accustomed to hearing regularly during the frequent marital arguments of my neighbours… "you do make me want to *urge* Ted Davy" and so forth.

Cornwall is the most southerly as well as westerly English county and in previous centuries was often substantially cut off. Until the late 18th century it had a separate Celtic language of its own and still maintains a propensity for strange words, pronunciations and grammatical constructions.

When I lived there some years ago the proprietress of a local corner store provided me regularly with rich examples of Cornish vernacular such as the description she offered of a very pretty girl who had just left her shop: "she sister to the boy who work up the electric at Camborne an' she no better than she belong to be" (ought to be).

My days of residence in West Cornwall coincided with my last years of playing serious cricket.

When I played for some years for the county side my colleagues liked to pretend I was authentically Cornish rather than a specially-registered 'blow-in' from another county and even offered to instruct me in how to talk like a true local.

However, just how difficult the latter would have been was brought home to me when listening to the following conversation between a Cornish player on tour and the captain of the other side. The latter congratulated our player on a brilliant run-out – praise our player modestly rejected.

"I jes picked un up an frawed it to the wicket-keep" our boy explained but several minutes later their captain was none the wiser.

"Are you saying something about *fraud*' the latter asked anxiously.

I suppose I should have explained that frawed meant throwed or even threw but the whole thing seemed too hard. Besides this the misunderstanding had a certain poetic or even surreal quality which one might secretly savour.

Regional idiosyncracies formerly contributed much more to life than we probably realised – often in ways we could never have imagined.

The Australian, 2009 commissioned but not published

INDEX OF NAMES